Southern Crafted

TEN NASHVILLE CRAFT BREWERIES

Dedicated to Making Sure the Beer Is Drinkin' Good

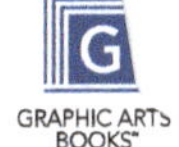

Additional Photography provided by Alex Barr, Andrea Behrends, Matt Hearn, and Justin Wright Photography.

ISBN: 978-1-943328-26- 0 (paperback)
ISBN: 978-1-943328-27-7 (e-book)
Library of Congress Control Number: 2015947331

Writer: Jeff Yeager
Designer: Candice Sweet
Creative Director: Terry Morrison
Project Manager: Hilary Ford

Published by Graphic Arts Books
An imprint of Turner Publishing Company
4507 Charlotte Avenue, Suite 100
Nashville, TN 37209
(615) 255-2665
www.turnerbookstore.com

Acknowledgments

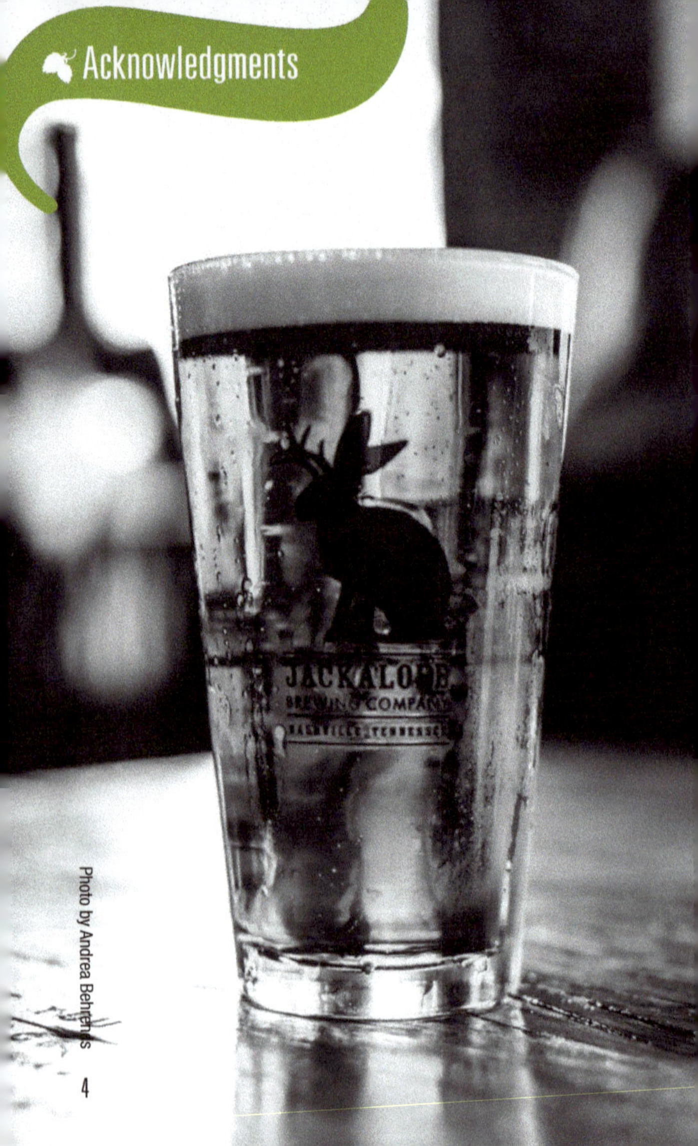

Photo by Andrea Behrends

A big thank you to all the people who helped make this book happen. The owners, founders, brewers, brew-masters, bartenders, and others from:

- Little Harpeth
- Black Abbey
- Blackstone
- Czann's
- Jackalope
- Yazoo
- Tennessee Brew Works
- Fat Bottom Brewing
- Turtle Anarchy
- Honky Tonk Brewery Co.

And any other people who were kind enough to take time out of their day to speak with us and feed us free beer. Cheers to all you wonderful folks! A special thanks to Neil for that gem of inspiration tying it all together.

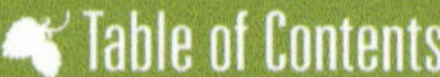

Photo by Justin Wright Photography

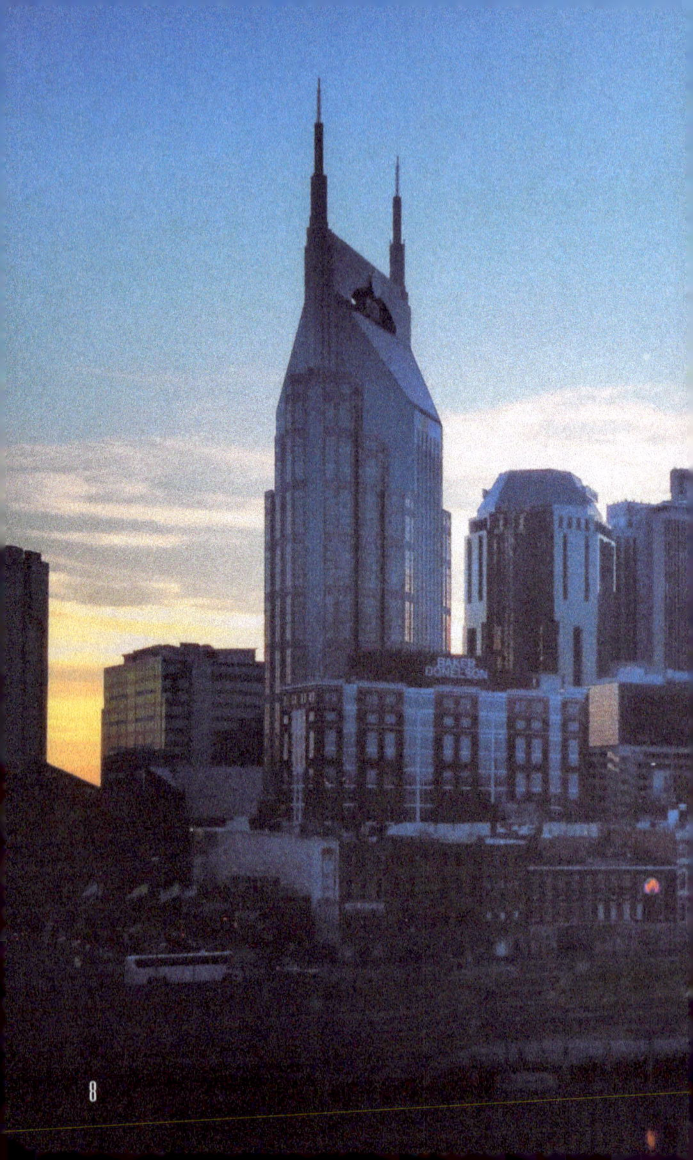
BAKER
DONELSON

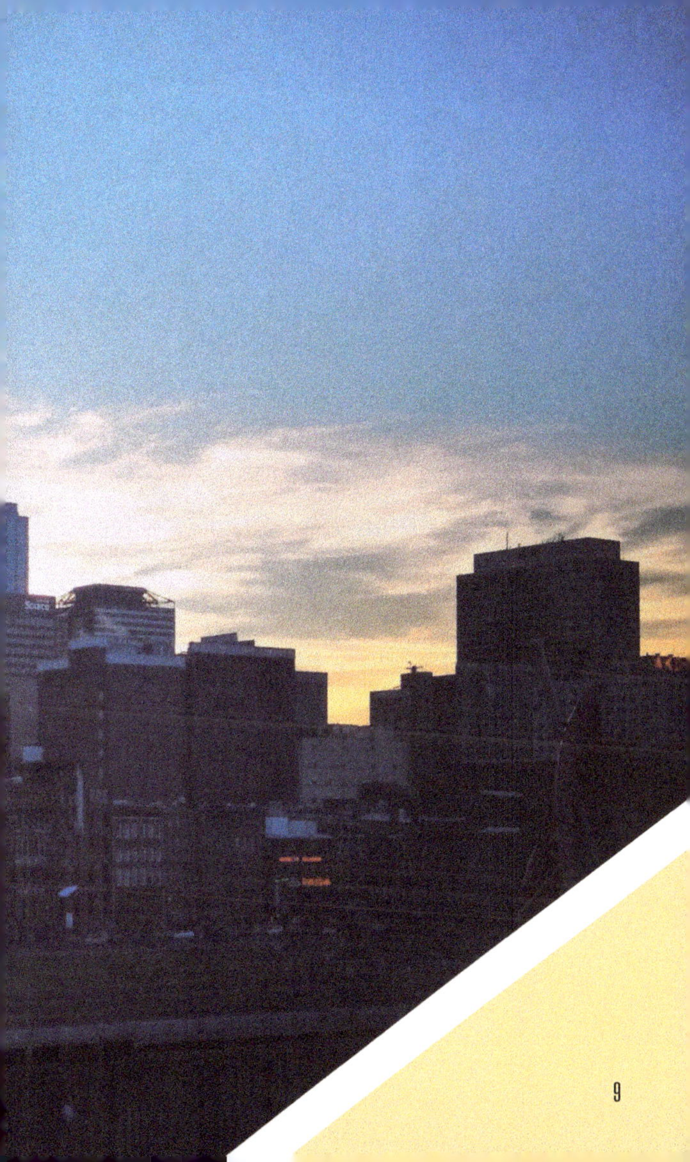

Craft Beer Goes South (in a Good Way)

Before we begin to dive into the people and places that make Nashville a shining beacon for casual beer fans and craft connoisseurs alike, let's travel back to a dark and ancient time when things were not so . . .

When the craft beer revolution started to gain national momentum around 2010 there were more than 1,750 craft breweries in the US. Fast-forward to 2014 and that number leaped the 3,400 mark. However, the majority of these fine houses of hops and malted barley were, and to this day still are, located in the Northwestern, Midwestern, and Northeastern regions of the country.

Why is that?

Four things . . .

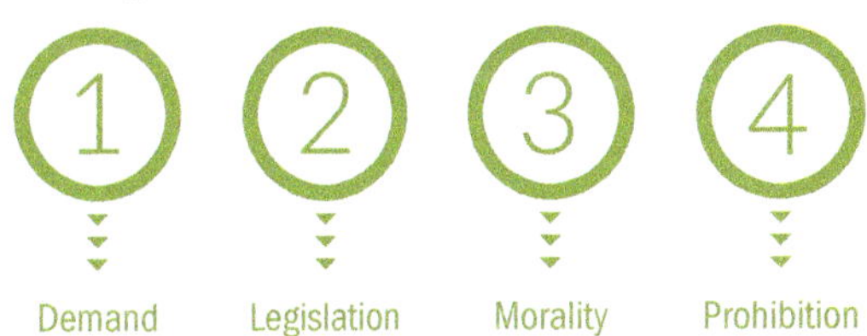

Yes, Prohibition, a law that was repealed more than eight decades ago, still has a lasting impact on beer production in the South.

The last three are intrinsically tied together. Prohibition, mostly considered a movement of morality, saw huge support in the Bible Belt and there is still a large Southern constituency that holds tight to this ideology.

For example, up until 2013, in Mississippi and Alabama, if you were brewing beer in the comfort of your own home, you were a fugitive from the law.

As for demand, if Budweiser, Miller, and Coors are the only options available to you, then why leave your comfort zone? The more successful craft brewers recognize this, making the South a market that historically has been better left untapped. But things are changing.

Cultivating the Nashville Craft Beer Scene

At a state level, Nashville floats freely above other Tennessee towns at sixteen breweries and climbing; Knoxville and Chattanooga are next with six each. In the last three years more than eight new breweries have taken root in Nashville. According to the Brewers Association, the city now also boasts one of the fastest-growing craft breweries in the United States as of 2012. So, suffice it to say, things are getting serious.

With other states in the region struggling mightily against the lingering bitterness of Prohibition, how has the Nashville craft beer scene matured so well?

Aside from the fact that making their own booze is somewhat ingrained in the fabric of Tennesseans, the easiest explanation is Tennessee realizes the greater economic benefits of craft brewing.

Though the Volunteer State has the highest beer tax in the nation, most legislation, as it applies to beer production, makes it a very proactive place for startup breweries. How so you ask? Consider these three things:

A modernized, stabilized beer tax.

An increase in maximum ABV% (Alcohol by Volume percentage, for the uninitiated).

The ability to self-distribute in their own county.

You can thank the members of the Tennessee Craft Brewers Guild (a nonprofit group based out of Nashville) for those first two items.

Add all that together with a booming economy and one of the fastest-growing metro areas in the nation, and it is pretty easy to see why Nashville makes a great location for craft brew startups.

But it is more than just politics. There is commerce and community behind this beast.

As a thriving center of economic boom, Nashville lends itself to entrepreneurship and local business. It also boasts a healthy tourism industry and possesses a young, adventurous demographic ready and willing to try new things. It also helps that at least once a month you can find some embodiment of a beer festival going on around town, which has given the national craft brewing community cause to pay attention.

The Nashville community, with its collective thirst for brews that are more pleasing to their palates, is but a microcosm in this surging universe of bubbly artisan beverages. A closer examination of the Nashville craft beer scene will show you it's strongest at its roots. And those roots go almost a decade deep, back to 1996, when the homebrew club Music City Brewers held its first meeting.

At the heart of the this club was a group of people passionate about the beer they drink, all wanting to brew something they themselves would enjoy and share it with their community. Of the ten breweries featured in this guide, five owners/founders were early members of the Music City Brewers.

Most of the brewers covered in this book—though they all have different styles, ambitions, and philosophies—all live to give beer drinkers something enlightened, something different. It's not about competing against each other or the likes of Budweiser, Coors, and Miller (well, maybe just a bit). But mostly it is about education. Showing people that they have other options, and those options are damn good.

For these craftsmen and women, every handle, bottle, or can that graces a bar, convenience store, or grocery store is a win for craft beer in Nashville. They are all in it together—from borrowing ingredients to lobbying for the city's official endorsement of the Brewery District—for the betterment of craft beer and for making sure the beer you get here is drinkin' good.

"Go South, craft beer! Go South!"

To evoke famed 19th-century author, journalist, politician, and craft beer fanatic Horace Greeley, the call "Go South, craft beer! Go South!" has been answered. And of the southern cities that have stepped up their craft brewery game, Nashville stands tall.

Now . . . to the breweries!

Black Abbey Brewing
2952 Sidco Dr
Nashville, TN 37204
P: 615.755.0070
www.blackabbeybrewing.com

Taproom Hours:
Wed-Fri: 3:30pm – 8:00pm
Sat: 12:00pm – 8:00pm
Sun: 12:00pm – 6pm

Blackstone Brewing
2312 Clifton Ave
Nashville, TN 37209
P: 615.320.9002
www.blackstonebrewery.com

Taproom Hours:
Wed-Fri: 4:00pm – 8:00pm
Sat: 12:00pm – 8:00pm
Sun: 2:00pm – 6:00pm

Blackstone Brewpub
1918 West End Ave
Nashville, TN 37203
P: 615.327.9969
www.blackstone-pub.com

Brewpub Hours:
Fri-Sat: 11:00am – 1:00am
Mon-Thurs: 11:00am – 12:00am
Sun: 12:00pm – 10:00pm

Czann's Brewing
505 Lea Ave
Nashville, TN 37203
P: 615.748.1399

Taproom Hours:
Thurs-Fri: 4:00pm – 8:00pm
Sat: 12:00pm – 8:00pm
Sun: 12:00pm – 6:00pm

Fat Bottom Brewing
800 44th Ave
Nashville TN 37209
P: 615.678.5715
www.fatbottombrewing.com

Taproom Hours:
Tues-Fri: 5:00pm – 10:00pm
Sat: 12:00pm – 10:00pm

Honky Tonk Brewing Co.
240 Cumberland Bend
Nashville, TN 37228
P: 615.742.9770

Taproom Hours:
Thurs-Fri: 12:00pm – 8:00pm
Sat: 12:00pm – 5:00pm

Jackalope Brewing
701 8th Ave S
Nashville, TN 37203
P: 615.873.4313
www.jackalopebrew.com

Taproom Hours:
Wed: 4:00pm – 8:00pm
Thurs: 4:00pm – 10:00pm
Fri: 4:00pm – 8:00pm
Sat: 12:00pm – 8:00pm
Sun: 2:00pm – 6:00pm

Little Harpeth Brewing
30 Oldham St
Nashville, TN 37213
www.littleharpethbrewing.com

Tap Room Opening
Late Summer 2015

Tennessee Brew Works
809 Ewing Ave
Nashville, TN 37203
P: 615.200.8786
www.tnbrew.com

Taproom Hours:
Wed-Fre: 5:00pm – 10:00pm
Sat: 2:00pm – 10:00pm
Sun: 2:00pm – 8:00pm

Turtle Anarchy Brewing
216 Noah Dr #140
Franklin, TN 37064
P: 615.595.8855
www.turtleanarchy.com

Taproom Hours:
Thurs-Fri: 5:00pm – 10:00pm
Sat: 4:00pm – 10:00pm

Yazoo Brewing
910 Division St
Nashville, TN 37203
P: 615.891.4649
www.yazoobrew.com

Taproom Hours:
Wed-Fri: 4:00pm – 8:00pm
Sat: 12:00pm – 6:00pm

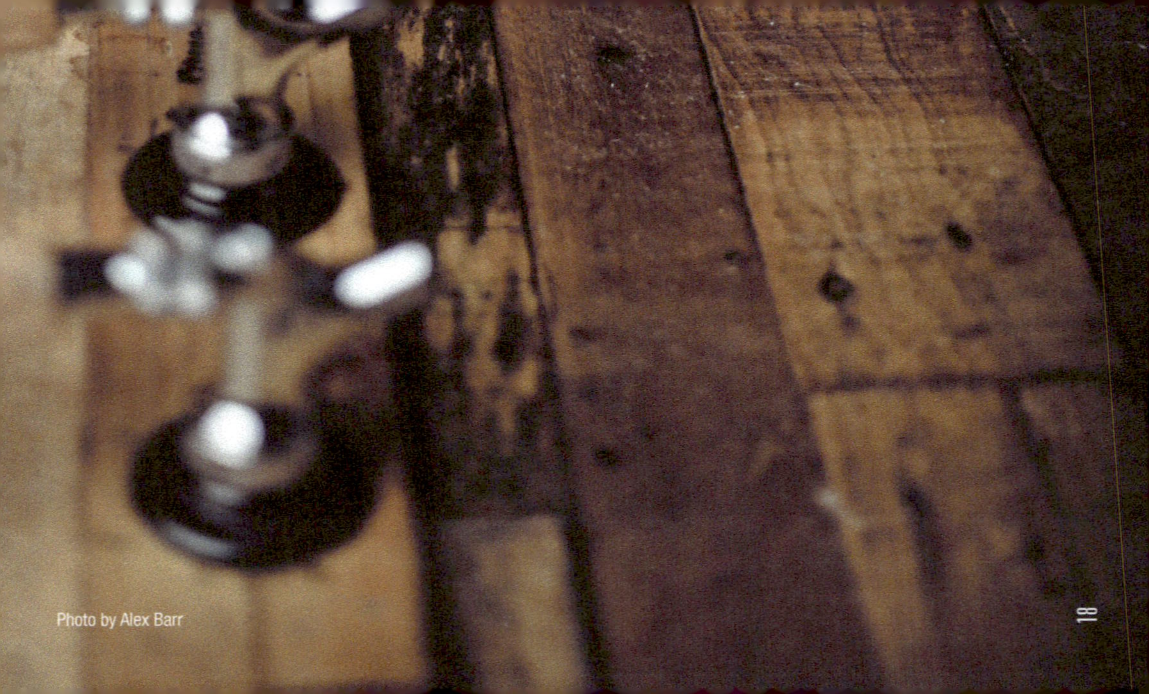

Photo by Alex Barr

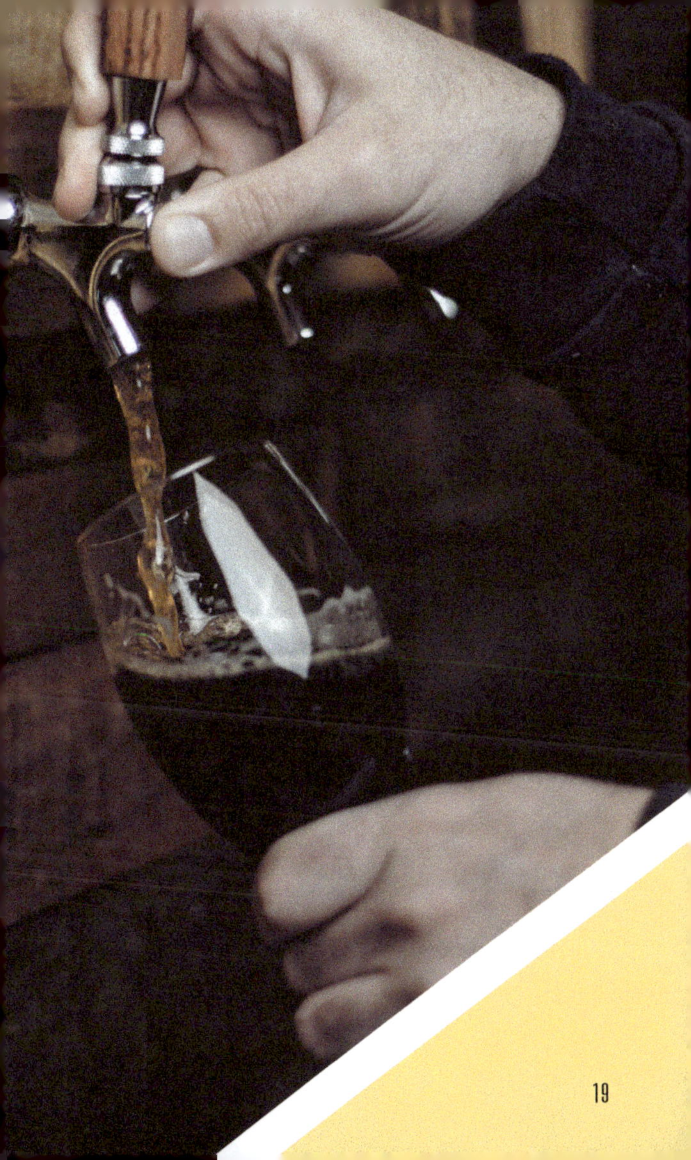

Little Harpeth Brewing Co.

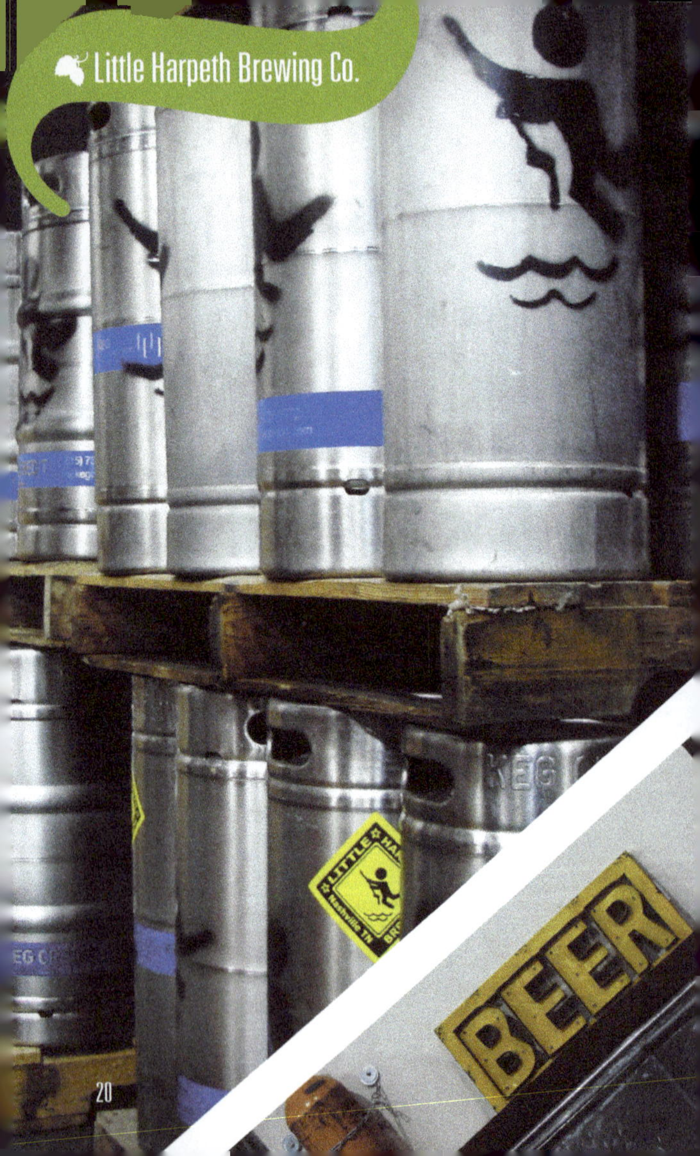

"We brew *great beer* for today and we grow great brewers for tomorrow."

The Story

Though a couple decades separate founder Michael Kwas and head brewer Steve Scoville, their dedication to well-crafted beers surpasses the limits of time and space. Indeed, if Einstein were alive today, he would love their beer. Kwas, who grew up in Nashville, spending many a hot summer day rope swinging into the Little Harpeth (hence the name), began home brewing in college, while Scoville, one of the early members of Music City Brewers, had been home brewing since 1998. Once Kwas's savvy business acumen combined with Scoville's mastery of the German-style lager brewing process, lightning struck, and Little Harpeth began to take root. In 2014 they rolled out their first keg.

One of the best brewpub views of downtown Nashville courtesy of Little Harpeth.

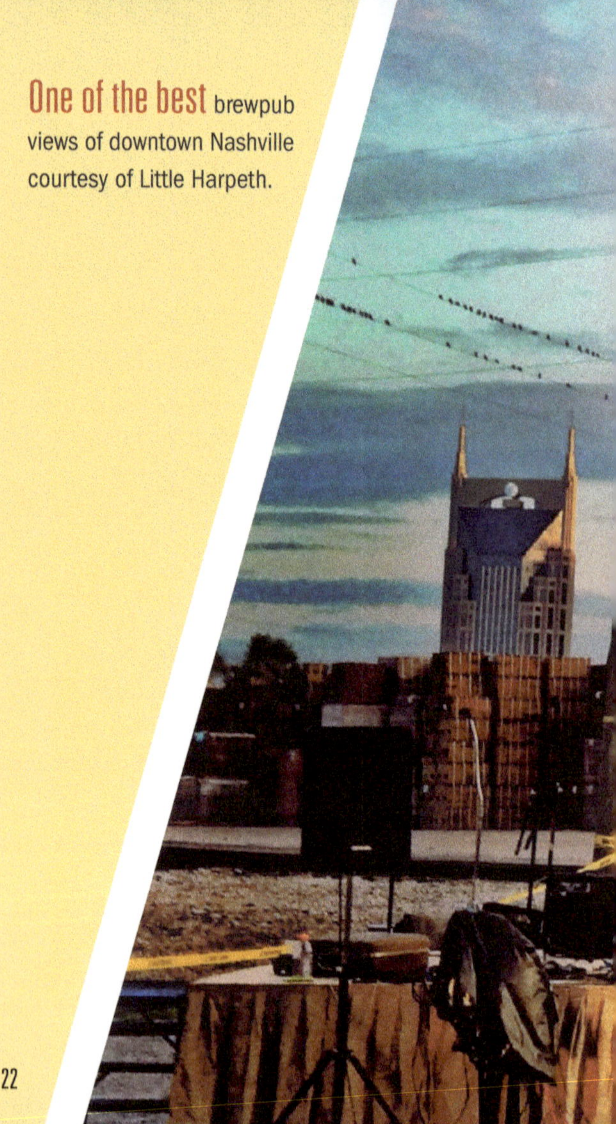

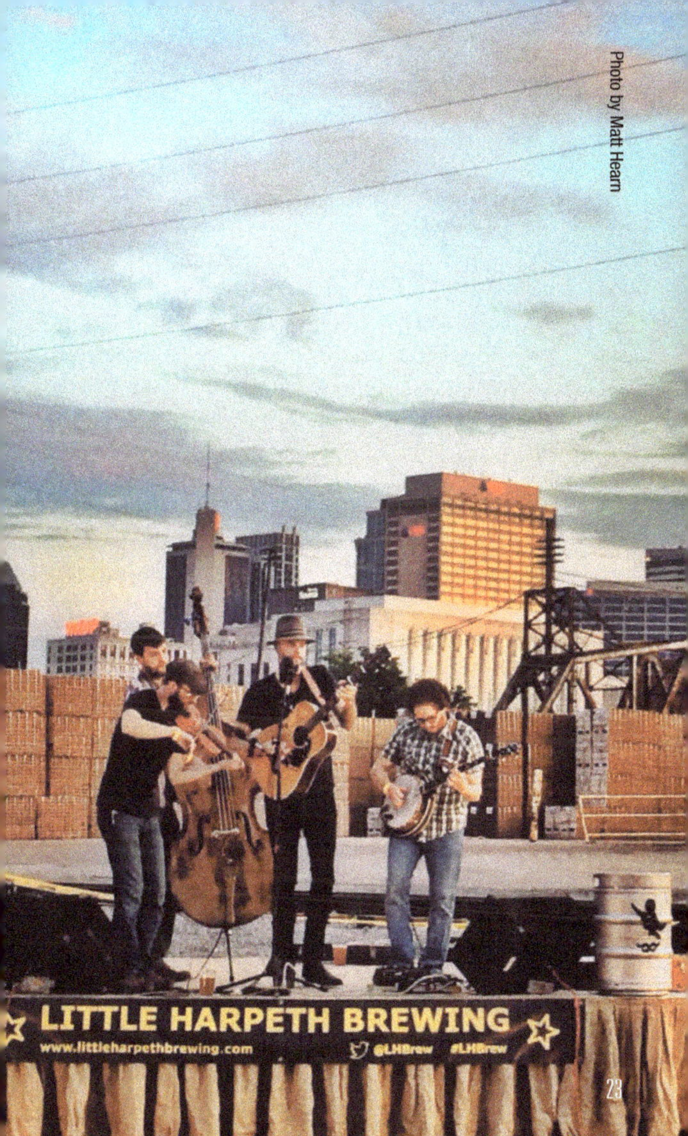

Photo by Matt Hearn

Keepin' the Beer Drinkin' Good

Like the yin and the yang, together Kwas (yin) and Scoville (yang) have created a dynamic craft brewery focused on delicious beer, education, and sustainability.

One of only four German-style lager craft breweries east of the Mississippi, Little Harpeth also doubles as an unconventional school for aspiring brewers. The doors are wide-open to volunteers wanting to work and learn; they are even given the chance to put their creations to the test using Scoville's vintage 1998 "brewing cart," a sort of centerpiece for the brewery itself.

With the exception of the big equipment, most everything in the brewery is recycled or repurposed. Their "green" efforts even extend all the way through their process. Eighty percent of their malt is produced without the use of fossil fuels and their steam boiler uses 40 percent less energy than other breweries. All this significantly reduces their carbon footprint.

Located on the banks of the Cumberland (definitely the best view of any brewery in this book), don't take Little Harpeth's rough and rugged industrial exterior for granted. Like Mom always said, it's what's on the inside that really matters. While Little Harpeth is making sure the beer is drinkin' good, they are also helping to further cultivate the Nashville craft beer scene through education and finding more sustainable ways for getting fine tasting suds into your glass.

LITTLE HARPETH BREWING
Nashville TN

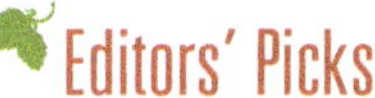

Editors' Picks

Chicken Scratch American Pilsner: (5.7% ABV, 38 IBU)

High Water Dunkle Lager: (6% ABV, 23 IBU)

Stax - Black Lager: (3.8% ABV, 40 IBU)

The Checklist

Taproom: Coming Soon

Bottles/Cans: Nope

Availability: Rutherford, Williamson, Sumner, Davidson, and Wilson counties . . . pretty much only in Middle TN

Website: www.littleharpethbrewing.com

What Brew Best Represents You?

Chicken Scratch American Pilsner
(5.7% ABV, 38 IBU) - The only commercially available American Pilsner in the world! Made with 30% locally grown, non-GMO, white hickory king heirloom corn, and America's only native hop variety. Light and flavorful with a sweet floral/herbal aroma.

@LittleHarpethBrewing

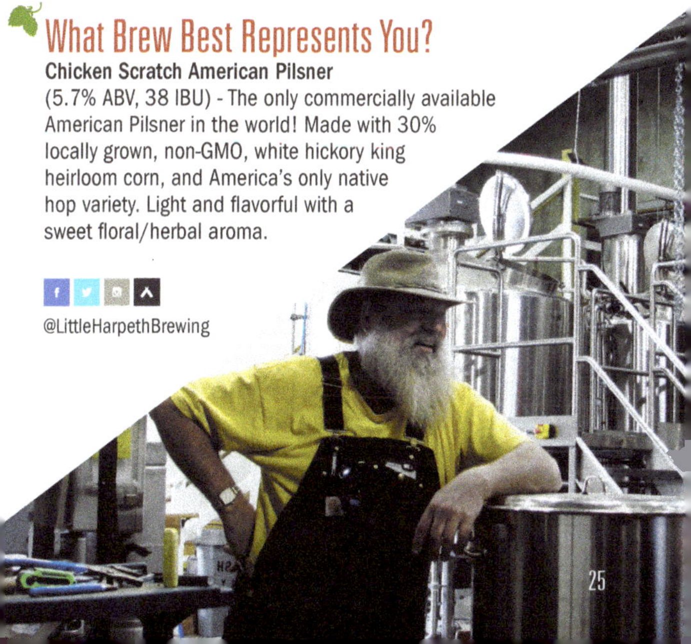

The Story

The aptly named Black Abbey was founded by Carl Meier and John Owen, two guys who are. . . . Well, we think Chris Chamberlain of the *Nashville Scene* put it best, ". . . not afraid to beat [an idea] to death until the very last bit of funny is shaken loose. From punny beer names to heavy metal theme parties to the hugely popular Beer and Hymn sing-alongs, Meier and Owen recognize that if drinking beer isn't fun, then really what's the point?"

Meier and Owen meet through the home brew club Antioch Sud Suckers (ASS), an offshoot of the Music City Brewers. After winning a silver medal in 2009 at a National Homebrew Competition, they began working on a business plan. Come September 2013, they rolled their first beer out the door and have been facilitating parties ever since.

"Created,
not made."

Keepin' the Beer Drinkin' Good

With pews lining the walls, gothic wrought iron lamps hanging from the vaulted ceilings, and stacks upon stacks of oak aging barrels, Black Abbey is one part monastery chapter house, one part German beer hall, and a whole heaping spoonful of craft beer fellowship.

Formerly an old Bible binding factory (fitting), Black Abbey takes its name from The Black Cloister, the monastery where Martin Luther sparked the Protestant Reformation. Once the brewery founders discovered Luther's wife, a former nun, brewed a Belgian ale comparable to their style of beer, it was all but decided. Plus, Black Cloister Brewing Company was just too hard to say after a few drinks.

The spirit of that Luther story is what drives Black Abbey to keep the beer drinkin' good, to keep it authentic craft beer from authentic people who care about their neighbors. You can see it in the names of their beers, like The Rose, named after the Lutheran Crest; or the POTUS Series, which pays tribute to the ol' Commander in Chief. It also comes through in the way they do business, such as collaborating with other local brewers and businesses to create special batches. For them, it's not about trying to win Best in Show. Yeah, they have won some awards, but what drives them is creating artisanal beers people will enjoy. Beers that are a reflection of who they are–super nerdy metal-heads who love good craft suds.

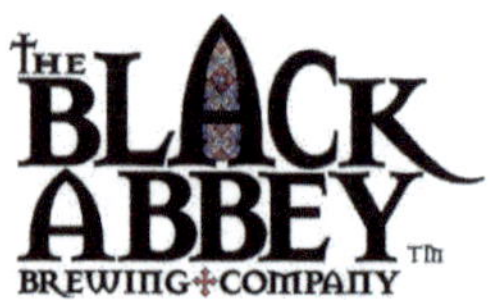

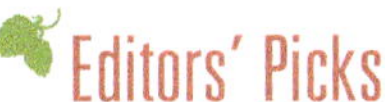

Editors' Picks

Chapter House Belgian Red: (5.7% ABV, 16 IBU)

The Special: (5.8% ABV, 13 IBU)

POTUS 44 Coffee Infused Porter: (5.5% ABV, 25 IBU)

The Checklist

Taproom: Yes

Bottles/Cans: 750ml bottles of barrel-aged goodness

Availability: The state of Tennessee, minus Shelby County

Website: www.blackabbeybrewing.com

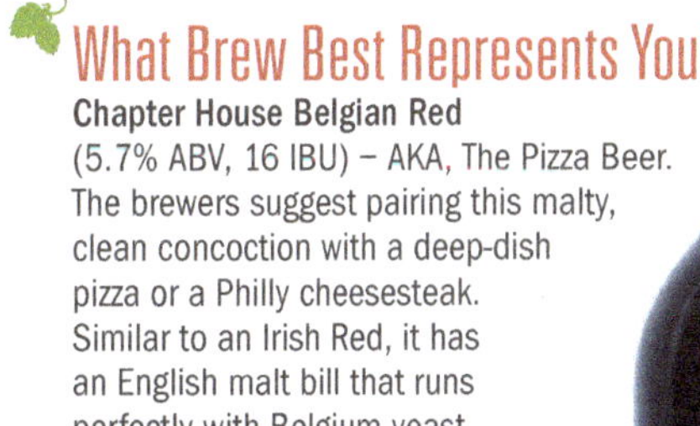

What Brew Best Represents You?

Chapter House Belgian Red

(5.7% ABV, 16 IBU) – AKA, The Pizza Beer. The brewers suggest pairing this malty, clean concoction with a deep-dish pizza or a Philly cheesesteak. Similar to an Irish Red, it has an English malt bill that runs perfectly with Belgium yeast.

@BlackAbbeyBrewing
@BlackAbbeyBrew

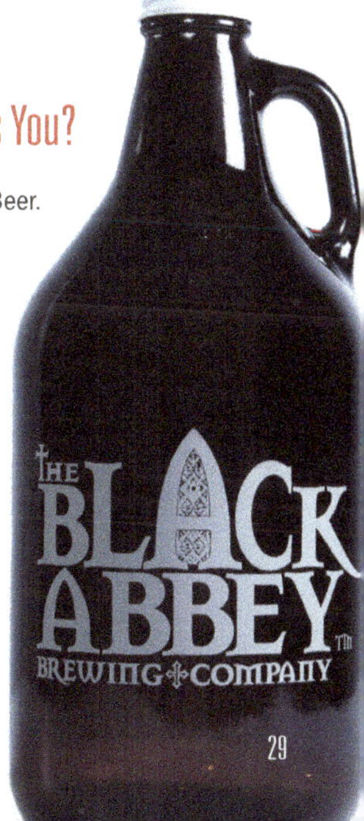

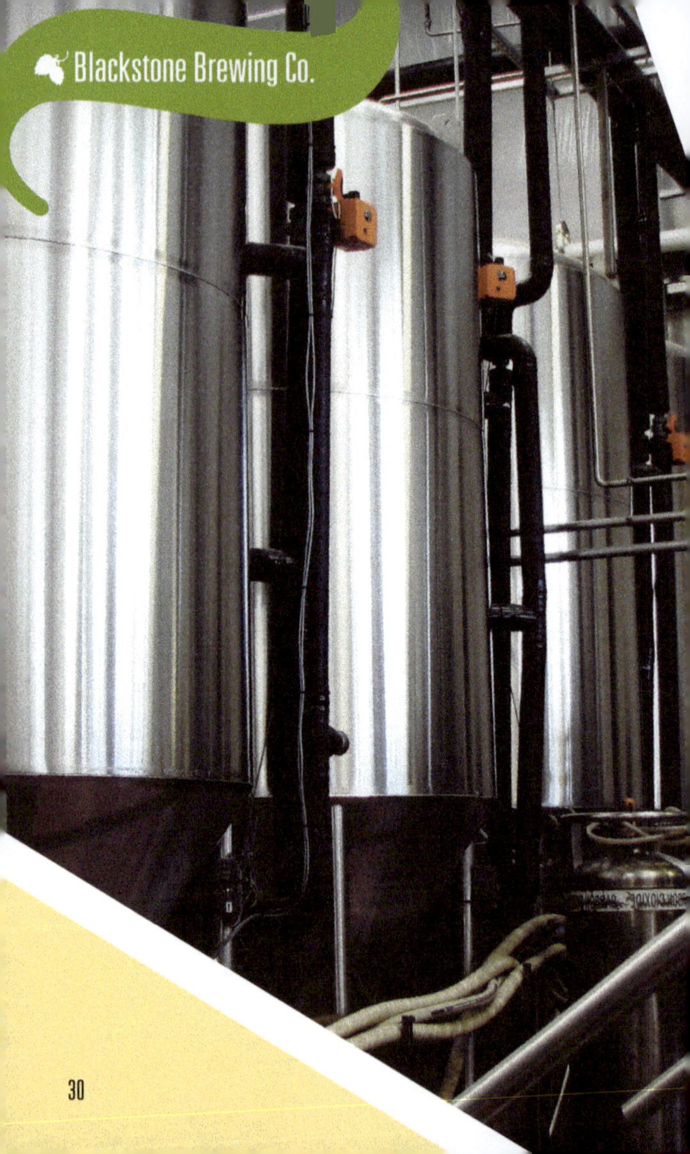
Blackstone Brewing Co.

The Story

First opened in 1994, Blackstone is one of Nashville's first craft breweries and has endured longer than any craft brewery in the city's recent history. According to data collected by the Brewers Association, it's also **the** fastest-growing craft brewery in the country–so it's kind of a big deal. But let's not get ahead of ourselves.

Kent Taylor–accountant by day, brewer of crafty goodness by night–started home brewing in the early '90s. Around that time he met his future business partner, Stephanie Weins. Through their shared love of craft beers and brewpubs, the two quickly became friends. After some arm-twisting, Taylor finally convinced Weins–who had an extensive background in restaurant management–that they needed to open a brewpub of their own. At that time, along with cargo shorts and grunge, opening a brewpub was still a novel idea. And in 1994 Blackstone brewpub became a reality. However, their current large-scale production facility did not open until 2010. With a state-of-the-art production warehouse and twenty years' experience under their belts, they quickly churned out their first beer in July 2011.

Keepin' the Beer Drinkin' Good

The Blackstone name is a bit like Six Degrees of Kevin Bacon. In an attempt to make a connection with the English beers that influenced their style, one of Taylor's clients suggested Blackstone, the name of a character in her son's Dungeons & Dragons® game. England has real dungeons and supposedly some dragons. And when they discovered there is an actual Blackstone, England, it was enough of a connection to justify the name.

While the brewpub definitely offers a tavernesque vibe, open all day and featuring an excellent menu of deliciously paired foods, it is the production facility that represents the culmination of Taylor and Weins's dream. Located in a warehouse in West Nashville, it is packed with all the "toys" you would expect to see in a big-time operation. An "expensive-ass" mill. A bottling line. A full lab with a spectrophotometer. Because if it makes better beer, it is worth it.

There is not enough space on these pages to cover everything Blackstone has done for craft brewing in Nashville. Suffice it to say, they've been keeping the beer drinkin' good longer than anyone else and it shows. Take their St. Charles Porter. Winner of eight Great American Beer Festival medals and two World Beer Cup medals, it is easily the best brown porter in the country, craft made in Nashville. But for all their laurels Taylor will tell you, it's not about beating out the other craft brewers in town. As Nashville's senior craft brewery it's about offering help to those local craft brewers who want it. Because if more local artisans can make better beer, and teach people to drink better beer, that is all the more craft beer fans in Nashville–and that's good for everyone.

"If it makes

better beer

make no compromises."

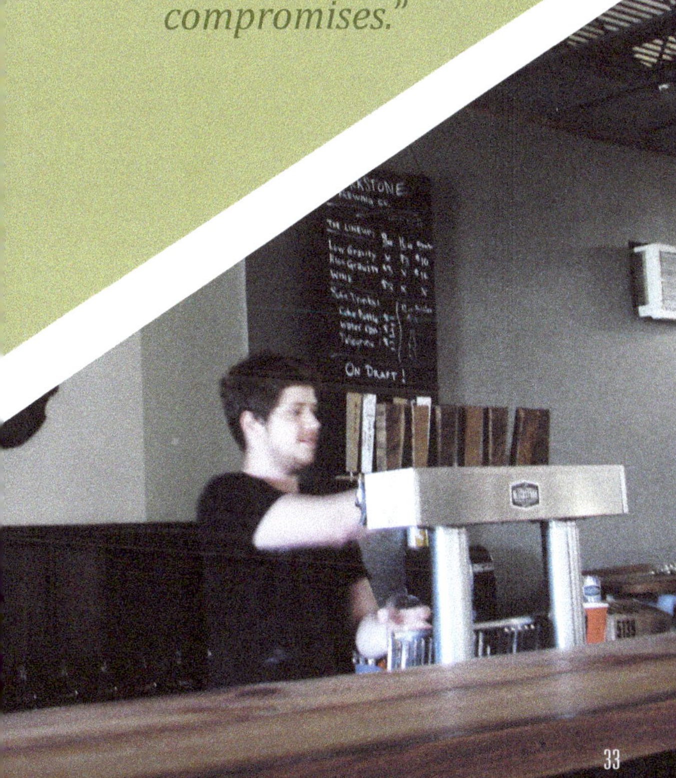

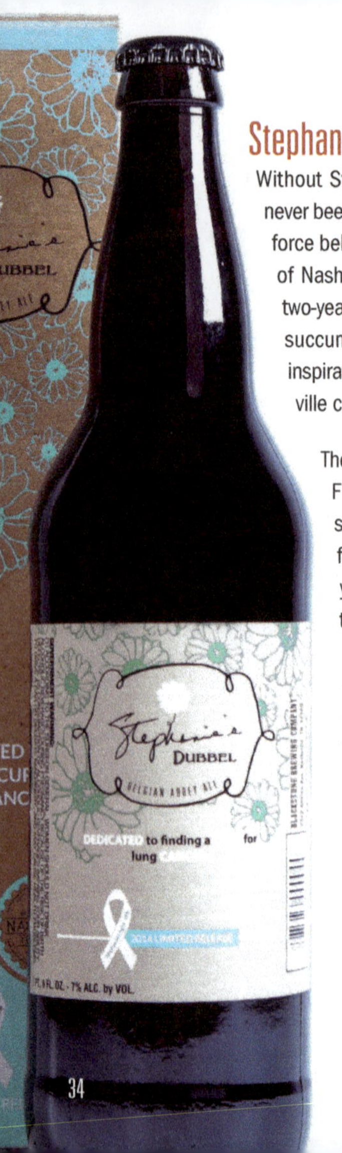

Stephanie's Fight

Without Stephanie Weins there would have never been a Blackstone. She was the driving force behind the business of brewing some of Nashville's most beloved suds. After a two-year battle, the Blackstone cofounder succumbed to lung cancer. She was an inspiration to hundreds, those in the Nashville craft beer scene and beyond.

The nonprofit organization Stephanie's Fight is dedicated to providing support for lung cancer research focused on finding a cure. In its first year Stephanie's Fight raised more than $25,000 and continues to make large contributions to funding lung cancer research. To contribute to Stephanie's Fight, visit www.stephaniesfight.org. For every $20 donated Blackstone is offering a 20oz. Bomber of its special release, Stephanie's Dubbel.

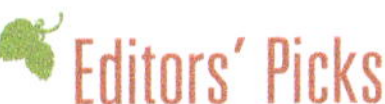

Editors' Picks

Chaser Pale German Kolsch: (5.2% ABV, 18 IBU)

St. Charles Brown Porter: (5.8% ABV, 34 IBU)

Nut Brown English Ale: (5.6% ABV, 23 IBU)

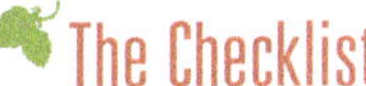

The Checklist

BLACKSTONE
BREWING COMPANY®
Nashville, Tennessee

Taproom: Yes

Bottles/Cans: Yes

Availability: All throughout the Volunteer State

Website: www.blackstone-pub.com

What Brew Best Represents You?

St. Charles Brown Porter

(5.8% ABV, 34 IBU) – Named after Taylor's son Charles, this award-winning beer is based off of one of Taylor's home brew recipes. A full-bodied beer, its heavy and sweet flavor is perfectly touched off with a tiny hint of raisin.

@BlackstoneBrew

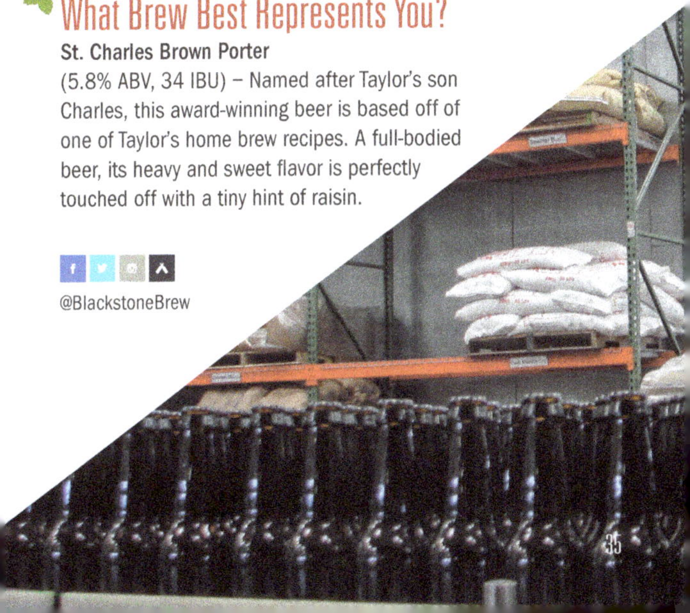

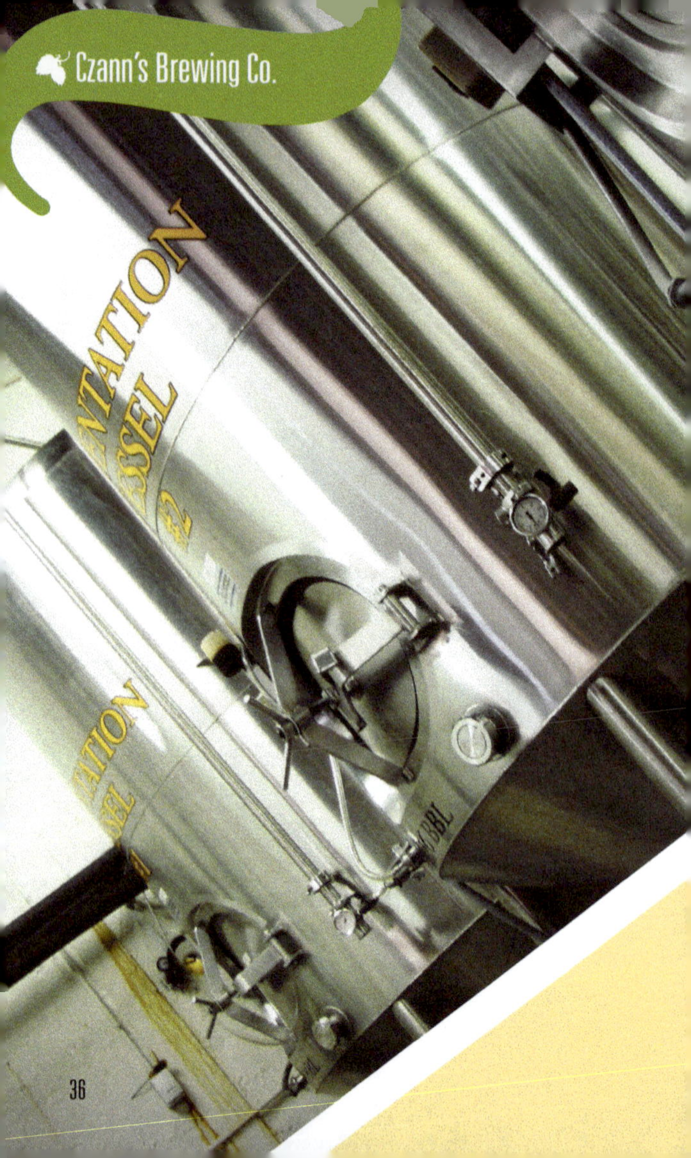

"masterly
designed beer"

The Story

We're moving from one of the largest breweries in Nashville to one of its smallest, but don't let that take anything away from Czann's *(pronounced "Zahnz")*. It is a Music City favorite well worth praise.

Head brewer and owner Ken Rebman first began brewing back in 1997. Not long after that he was seriously hit by the brewer's bug; symptoms included brewing every other weekend, an expansive database of home brew recipes, a three-year stint as the Music City Brewers' Treasurer, and a new home search centered around finding more brewing space. Along with this *ailment* came another problem common amongst most avid home brewers—a lot of beer, but not enough people to drink it. Soon Rebman began hosting beer parties and guests began suggesting he open his own brewpub. The brewery opened for wholesale business in 2012, and in 2014, Czann's—Rebman's home away from home—opened its doors to the public.

Keepin' the Beer Drinkin' Good

With no aspirations of becoming huge, Czann's is basically Rebman's basement relocated to an old 1940s repair shop just outside of Downtown Nashville's commercial center. Somewhere he could share his brews with a wider audience—away from where he sleeps.

The first in our venture across Nashville's Brewery District, this one-man show is not out to conquer the craft beer world or lay claim to the top spot in Tennessee. What Czann's strives for is approachable artisan beers. The key to that, Rebman says, are quality ingredients. In a coincidence as quaint as the owner, the name Czann's ties together Rebman's proclivity for superior ingredients with his ancestry, thus French malts, German hops, and American yeast. Expensive to make, but drinkin' good. Continuing on that path, Czann's is also a *frankenword*, combining his mother's maiden name, Czora, and his name, Rebman. Throw in props to Postimpressionist painter Paul Cézanne and you get Czann's, artfully crafted beers.

All quirky naming conventions aside, Czann's isn't about shocking the taste buds with something off-the-wall. The goal is accessible beers with a twist; similar, but different. It is Nashville craft beer education at its grassroots. As evident through its dedicated fan base, the "Drinkers Club," the brewery is a beacon for locals and visitors alike. A place where all are welcome to pull up a stool, share a pint with the owner, and enjoy a cordial introduction to craft beer in Nashville.

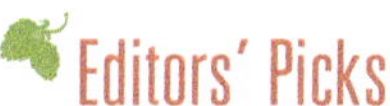

Editors' Picks

Blonde Belgium Ale: (4.25% ABV, 18 IBU)

Old School IPA: (6.2% ABV, 53 IBU)

Pale Ale: (5.25% ABV, 38 IBU)

The Checklist

Taproom: Yes

Bottles/Cans: No

Availability: Davidson County

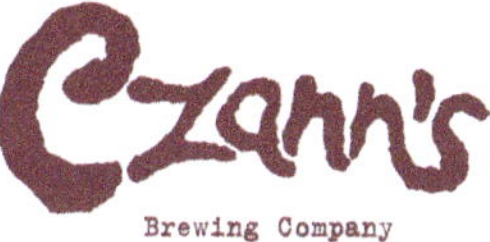

What Brew Best Represents You?

Blonde Belgium Ale

(4.25% ABV, 18 IBU) – Despite its complexity, using a whooping five different malts to create its full-profile flavor, this beer offers a great smooth taste with a light finish—perfect for a sunny day on the porch.

@Czanns

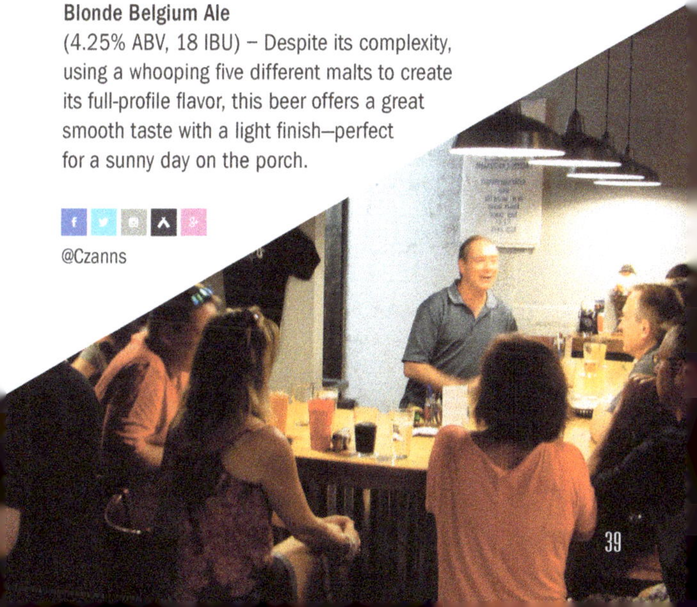

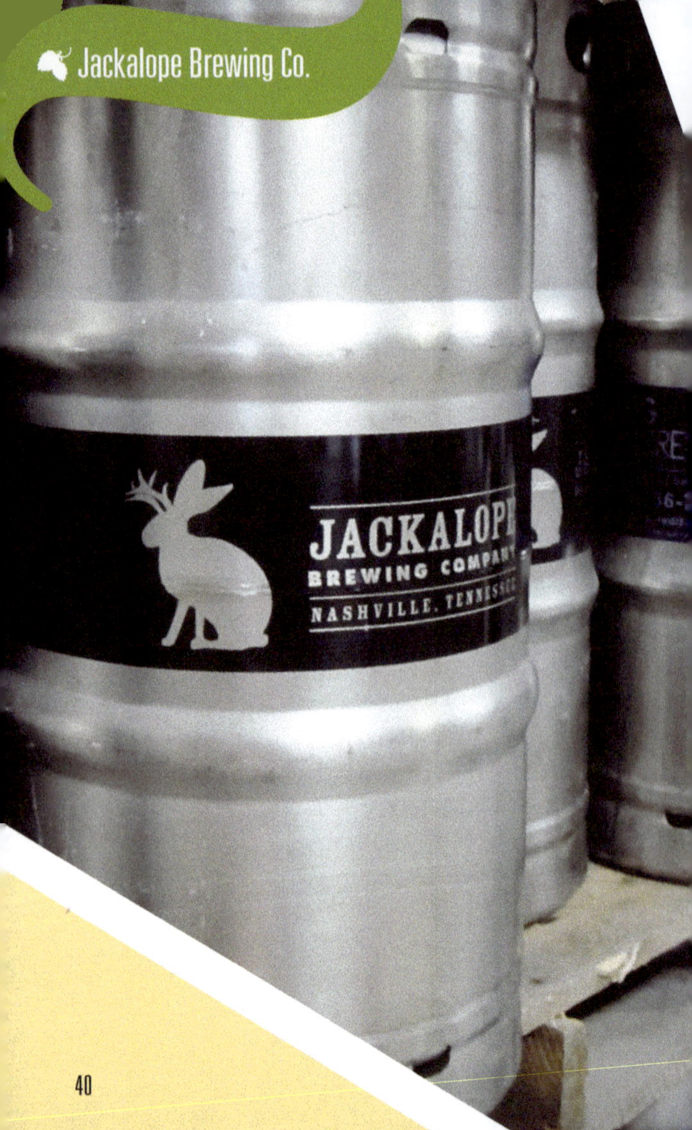
JACKALOPE
BREWING COMPANY
NASHVILLE, TENNESSEE

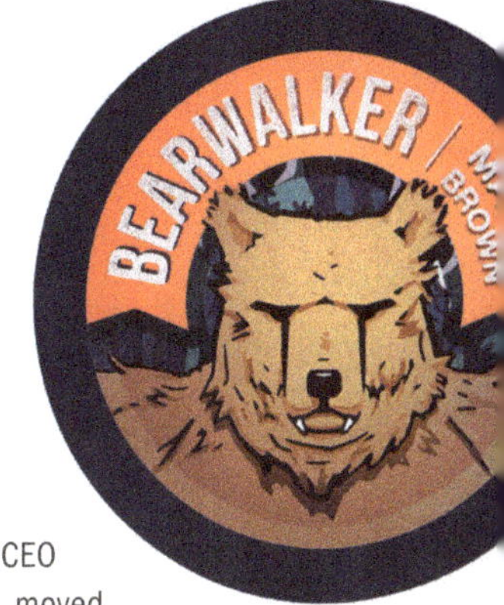

The Story

Hailing from Vermont, Jackalope CEO and cofounder Bailey Spaulding moved to Nashville in 2006 to study law at Vanderbilt University. It didn't take her very long to discover Nashville's craft beer scene was lacking. For someone from Vermont, this is akin to walking into a pancake factory that has never heard of maple syrup.

While law school trudged onward she began home brewing on her own, often finding herself thinking more about craft beer than practicing law. Before she knew it, Spaulding and her friend Robyn Virball, whom she had met while studying abroad in Scotland, were working on a brewery business plan. During planning Spaulding turned down a final-round interview with a legal NGO (nongovernmental organization). It was at that point the dream of Jackalope started to become an exciting reality. In 2009 she met Steven Wright, Jacaklope-fan-turned-intern-turned-head brewer. Just two years later, May 2011, they opened shop.

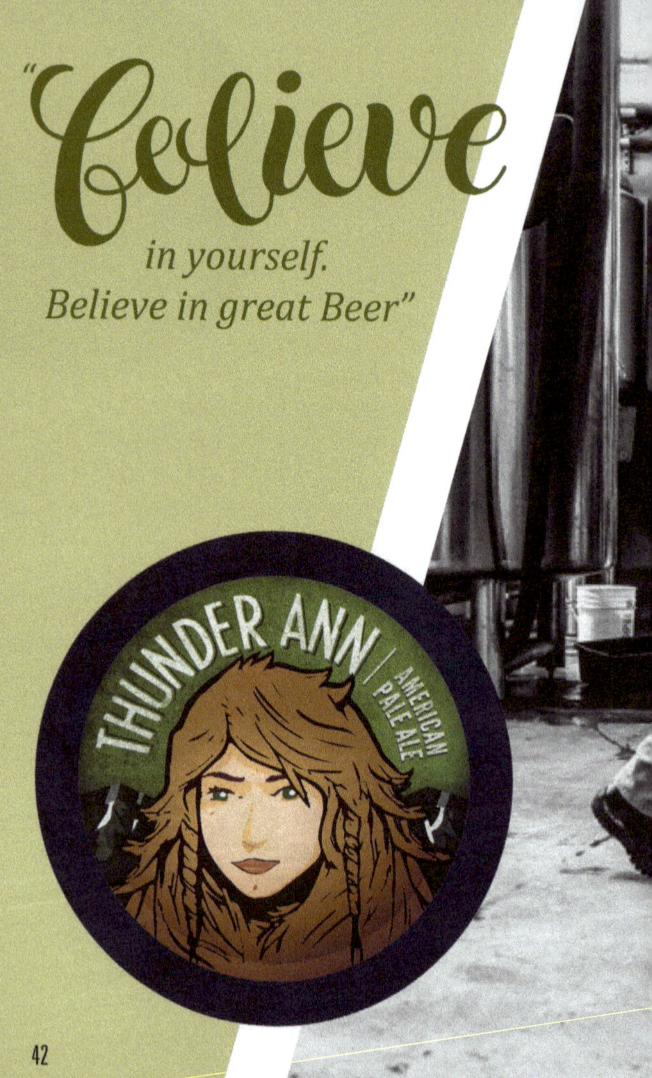
"Believe
in yourself.
Believe in great Beer"
THUNDER ANN
AMERICAN
PALE ALE

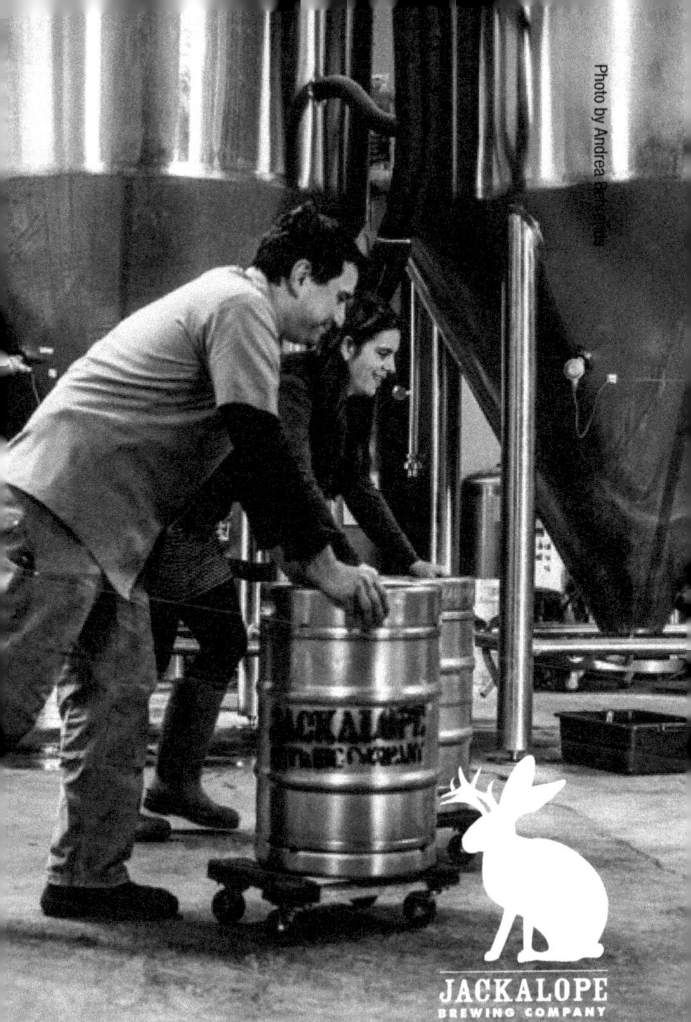

Photo by Andrea

Keepin' the Beer Drinkin' Good

When Jackalope opened its doors there were only two craft breweries in town. In about three years, ten more would pop up. Trendsetters? Maybe. A finger on the pulse of Nashville's dynamically growing community? Yes.

The second brewery in our tour through Nashville's Brewery District is but a stone's throw away from one of Nashville's most up-and-coming downtown areas. Jackalope is symbolic of the city's progressive nature and its thriving communal spirit. What they do reflects that spirit, from carefully crafted beers that speak to the varied Nashvillian palates to somewhat polarizing seasonals tied in with charitable causes. Their recipe to keeping the drinkin' good follows as so: a generous helping of mythically inspired creativity, a few handfuls of Vermontiness–a cultural respect for craft beer–and the idea that beer should be made with care, integrity, and joy, while giving something back to the community that supports it.

Their crafts epitomize that recipe. Like Bearwalker, named after a Canadian shapeshifter/sorcerer/wearbear, or Spruce Beersteen, a beer brewed in support of Nashville's W.O. Smith School, a nonprofit whose mission is to provide children from low-income families easy access to musical instruction. It is even alive in their building, which they share with the ZolliKoffe coffee shop, creating an urban meeting space open to the public throughout the day.

Jackalopes inspire. Always a fan of jackalopes, Spaulding owned a T-shirt that featured the supposed mythical creature with the text "Believe in Yourself." The good people at Jackalope Brewing Company take that slogan to heart. They believe in themselves. They believe in great beer. They also believe in their community, and it shows.

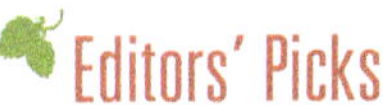

Editors' Picks

Bearwalker Maple Brown Ale: (5.1% ABV, 32 IBU)

Thunder Ann APA: (5.5% ABV, 37 IBU)

Leghorn Rye IPA: (6.0% ABV, 65 IBU)

The Checklist

Taproom: Yes

Bottles/Cans: Yes

Availability: Nashville, Murfreesboro, Clarksville, Chattanooga, Sewanee

Website: www.jackalopebrew.com

What Brew Best Represents You?

Spruce Beersteen Black IPA, Seasonal
(6% ABV, 67 IBU) – A slightly floral start touched off by spruce tips makes us want to cuddle up to this delicious favorite every fall. Plus, they throw a big party featuring local bands jamming out Bruce Springsteen covers on its release, so why not?

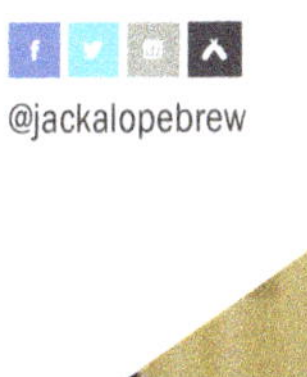

@jackalopebrew

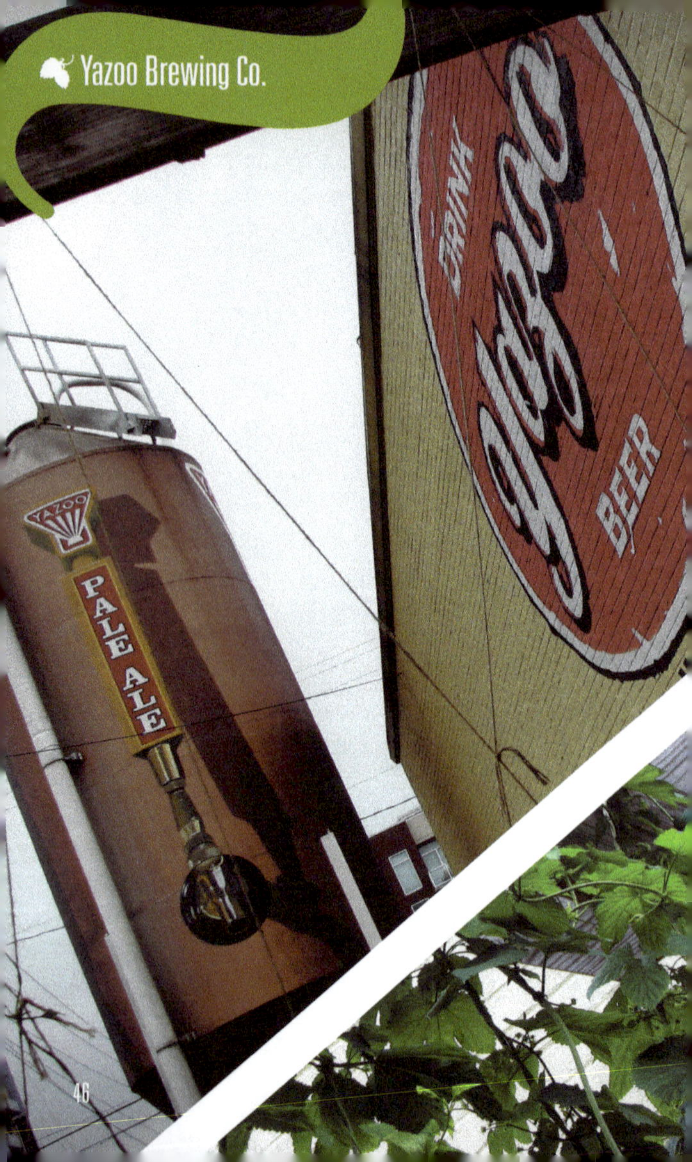
YAZOO
PALE ALE
DRINK
BEER

The Story

Linus Hall began brewing while he and his wife attended college in Virginia. After graduating in 1996 he moved to Nashville and took an engineering job with Bridgestone. Since making tires more round wasn't exactly fulfilling his creative juices, he continued to brew beer at home. At this time he was also a highly active member of the Music City Brewers.

As young couples often do, they attended many parties where Linus would bring his own beer. The beer, which was a much more popular conversation piece than the hottest tire technology, prompted people to suggest he look into the beer business. After Linus talked the subject to death, Lila, like any good wife, told him to either shit or get off the pot. Linus opted for the former.

After attending Siebel World Brewing Academy in Chicago, Hall got some hands-on experience interning at Brooklyn Brewery. Upon moving back to Nashville, the Halls opened their first location at Marathon Music Works in 2003. After experiencing exponential growth in 2010 they moved into their current space seated in Nashville's popular Gulch district.

"More isn't better, but getting better is better."

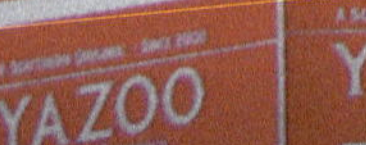

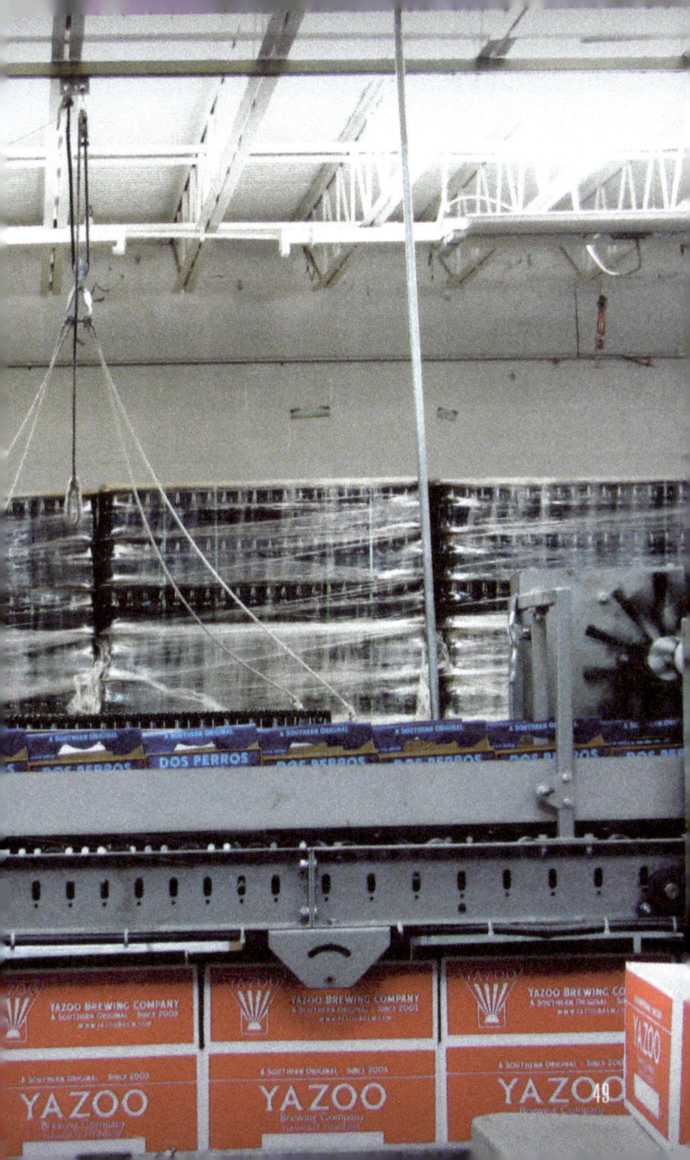
A SOUTHERN ORIGINAL
DOS PERROS
YAZOO BREWING COMPANY
A SOUTHERN ORIGINAL · SINCE 2003
A SOUTHERN ORIGINAL · SINCE 2003
YAZOO
Brewing Company

Keepin' the Beer Drinkin' Good

Tennessee's biggest brewery is 100 percent owned and operated by two high-school sweethearts from Vicksburg, MS, who married on the banks of the Yazoo River, the Mississippi River tributary from where the brewery claims its name.

All around Nashville, and most of Tennessee, Yazoo isn't necessarily competing for taps handles. Yazoo lives in Nashville's top bars, restaurants, and venues because people drink it; because it helps those businesses pay their bills. It's a bit of a Nashville staple.

From the onset they were never out to be the top dog in town. And it is not about keeping up with the Joneses of the craft brew nation. They simply focus on providing their peeps with really good beer.

Imagine if you got the same garlic mashed potatoes at every restaurant you visited. How bad would that suck? Now consider their Embrace the Funk series, featuring a beer that blends three different beers aged in three different wine barrels with Belgian Candi Sugar, blackberries, and merlot grapes. Never before have you had beer that tastes as divine. But sorry craft beer lovers worldwide, Embrace the Funk is a taproom exclusive, only available in Nashville. See? It always comes back to giving the hometown crowd the best tasting stuff.

Nashville is a drinking town, so it isn't Yazoo's top goal to crank out a version of whatever happens to be popular at the time, but to offer the drinking population thoroughly thought-out craft beers that are simply drinkin' good, beer that is synonymous with what Nashville stands for—a uniquely magical gem of creativity, ingenuity, and craftiness abutting the Cumberland River.

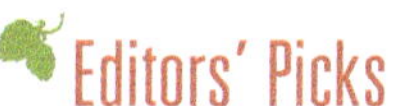

Editors' Picks

Gerst Amber Ale: (5.1% ABV, 11 IBU)

Onward Stout (Dry Stout): (3.8% ABV, 35 IBU)

Yazoo Pale Ale: (5.8% ABV, 47 IBU)

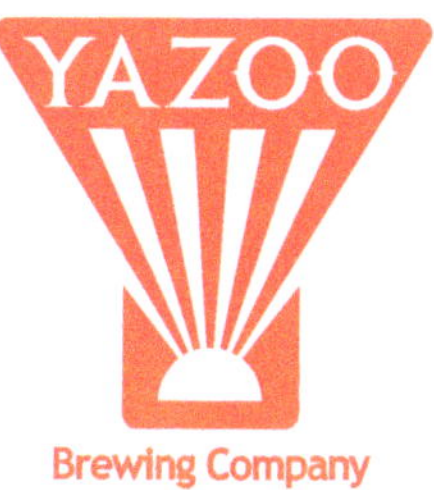

The Checklist

Taproom: Yes

Bottles/Cans: Yes

Availability: Tennessee and Mississippi

Website: www.yazoobrew.com

What Brew Best Represents You?

Yazoo Pale Ale

(5.8% ABV, 55 IBU): Exploding on the palate with a citrus and herbal hop aroma and a flavor that gives this take on an American classic a kick in the pants, this piece of craftsmanship features a full profile of English Pale, Munich, Vienna, and Crystal malts.

@YazooBrewing

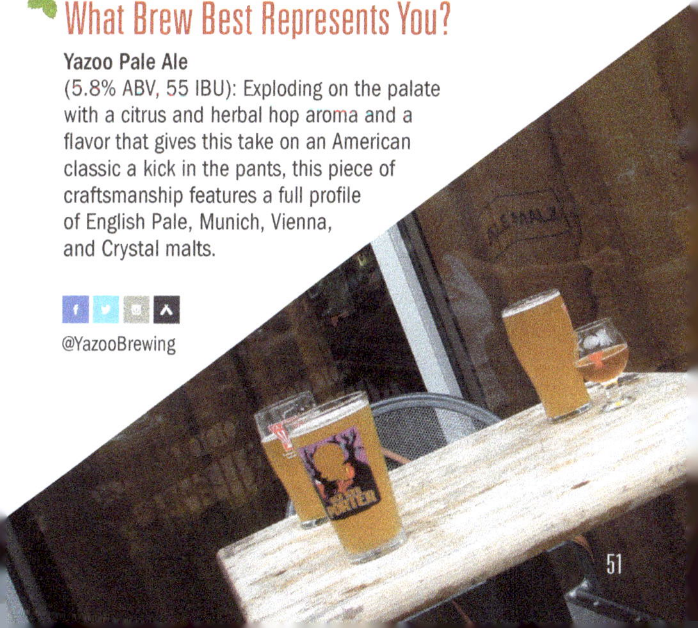

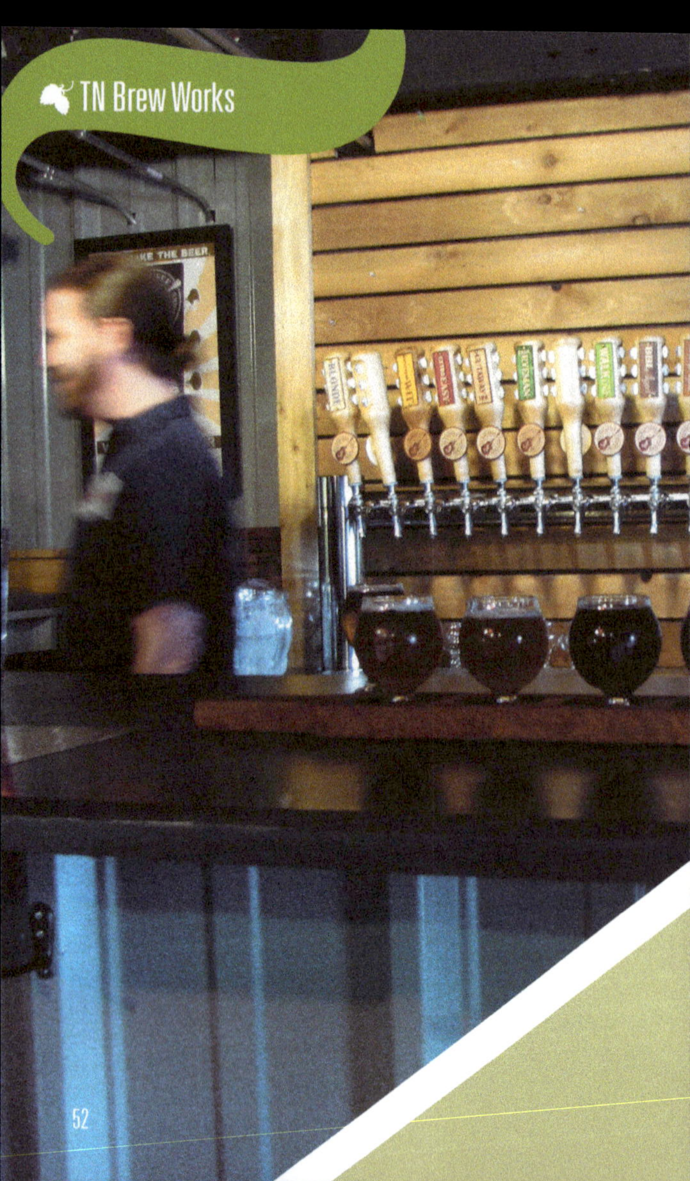

"finely tuned Craft Beers"

The Story

When Tennessee Brew Works founder Christian Spears's career in finance took him around the world, he developed a taste for good beer. But it wasn't until 2006, when Spears sampled his friend's Oatmeal Porter, that he realized it was possible to brew good beer at home. Then and there the brewer's seed was planted.

In 2007 Spears left the finance world to do volunteer work in India and Guatemala. His experience in those countries led him to an epiphany: wealth reallocation does little for the world; he needed to make something that mattered.

A few years later Spears moved to Nashville. With a strong support group of family, friends, and investors (all from TN) at his back, he and his friends decided that the best way they could contribute to the greater good of society was by making really great beer. In 2011 Spears and his crew finally decided if they were going to do this, they better do it right. After seeking out advice from a couple of mentors with some deep experience in the production biz, and with a bit more enthusiasm than expected, TN Brew Works rolled out its first beer in 2013.

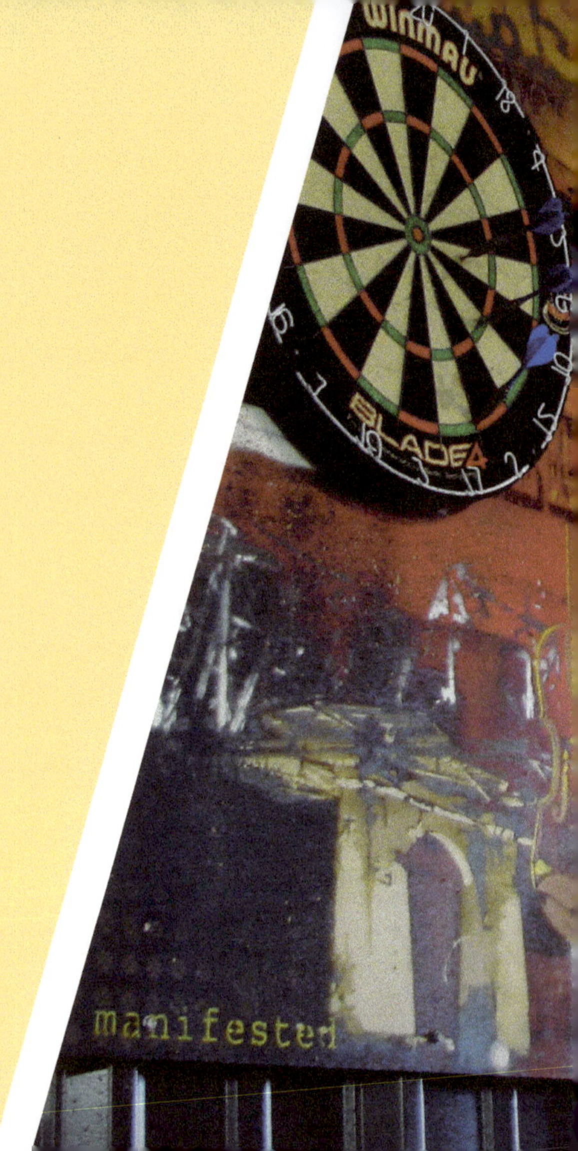
WINMAU
BLADE4
manifested

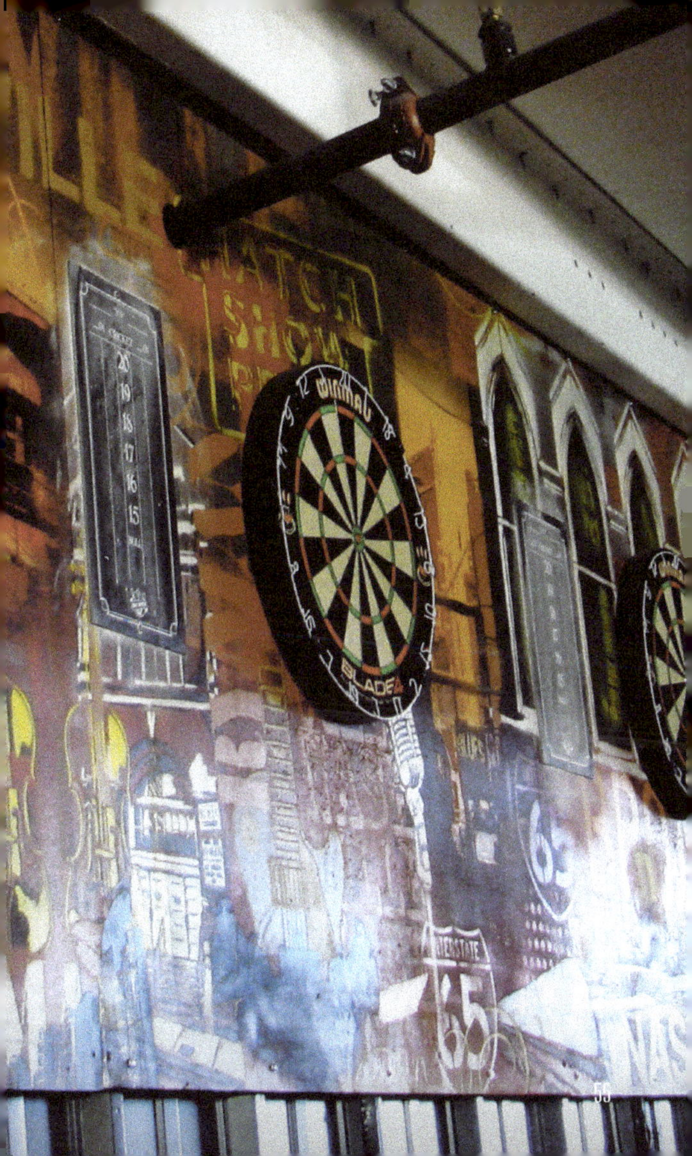

Keepin' the Beer Drinkin' Good

With a taproom that overlooks one of the cleanest production facilities you'll find south of the Mason-Dixon line, it's clear that the people at Tennessee Brew Works strive to make starkly obvious the connection between a lovingly crafted product and its source. The space revolves around that tie to localness. Like their Basil Ryeman® Farmhouse Ale and the seasonal Natchez Pale Ale, which both source ingredients from Bloomsbury Farm, just a few miles south down I-24, or their Country Roots Sweet Potato Stout®, sweet potatoes courtesy of Delvin Farms in College Grove, TN.

Tennessee Brew Works works hard to pair great beer with delicious food and fun to ensure that not only is the drinkin' good, but the experience is unmatched. Their head brewer has a PhD in microbiology, so you definitely know the beer is clean. And their all-star chef pairs every menu item, offering visitors a guide to taste bud Nirvana. Over there, a pair of architects work on a Jenga tower, while a couple of math geniuses across the way are dueling wits in a game of Connect Four. And every so often, for those needing a little detox after a night of drinkin' good, they can stop by Tennessee Brew Works for a yoga session capped off with a delicious and semi-nutritious "Beerboucha" (part craft beer, part kombucha; both made in-house).

It is definitely a production facility first and foremost, but you can't outsource its unique vibe or end product. You will never see people more happy to be working in a factory. Because what they do connects the community by helping build a strong foundation for craft beer in Nashville.

Editors' Picks

Southern Wit®: (5.14% ABV, 14.5 IBU)

Country Roots®: (5.5% ABV, 30 IBU)

Basil Ryeman®: (6.25% ABV, 28 IBU)

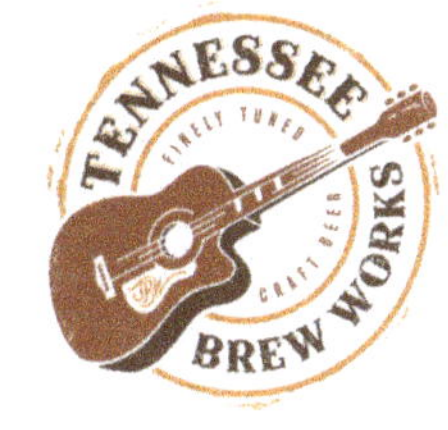

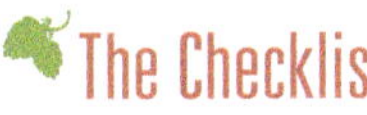

The Checklist

Taproom: Yes

Bottles/Cans: Yes

Availability: Memphis, Middle TN, and Knoxville

Website: www.tnbrew.com

What Brew Best Represents You?

Basil Ryeman Farm House Saison

(6.25% ABV, 28 IBU) – Thai basil locally sourced and rye malts team up to deliver an approachable but complex brew with hints of pepper and fennel. Chef Jay recommends pairing it with Italian, Thai, or grilled meats.

@TNBrewWorks

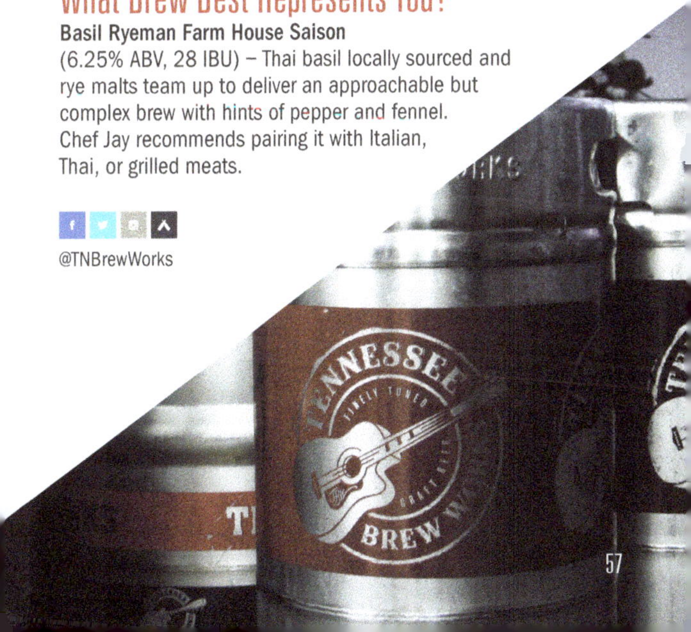

The Story

Born and raised in East Nashville, Fat Bottom founder Ben Bredesen has been a student of the brewer's craft for more than thirteen years. To this day he still brews beers at home. Many of their current offerings were taken from his earlier home brewing days, albeit slightly improved upon.

Before starting Fat Bottom, Bredesen, the son of former Tennessee Governor Phil Bredesen, worked for a software marketing company serving Nashville's booming health care industry. However, his passions were not seeded in wading through endless lines of code, but plunging headfirst into lovingly crafted blends of malt, barely, and hops. When it finally came to a head he left the software biz to focus on brewing beer full-time.

Bredesen himself constructed most of the East Nashville brewery, including the bar and the brew house. He added a full restaurant and opened up in 2011 in his old neighborhood. For now, Bredesen can ride his bike to work. Once they move to their new location across town with an expanded taproom, beer garden, and separate production facility, he might need to find a less exerting mode of transportation.

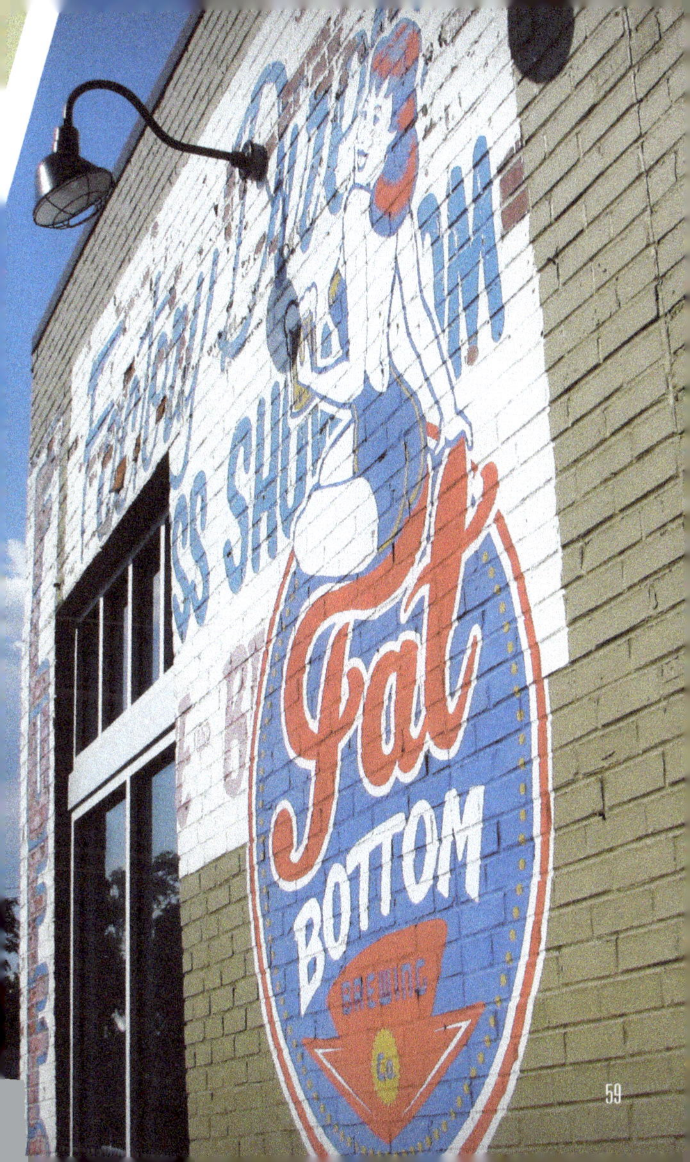
Fat
BOTTOM
BREWING
Co.

Photo by Alex Barr

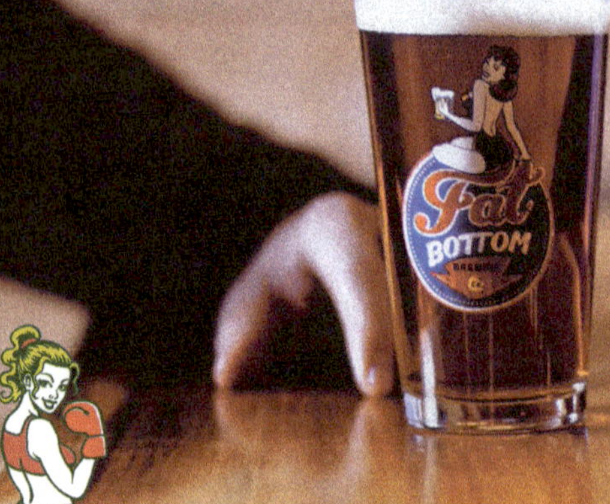

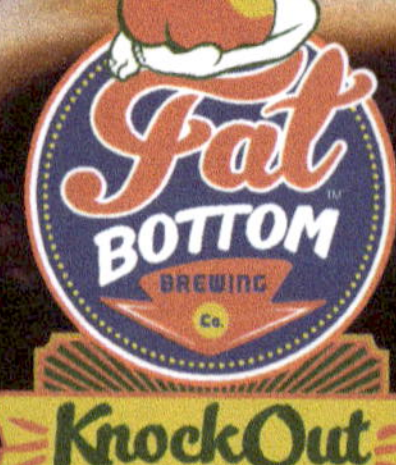

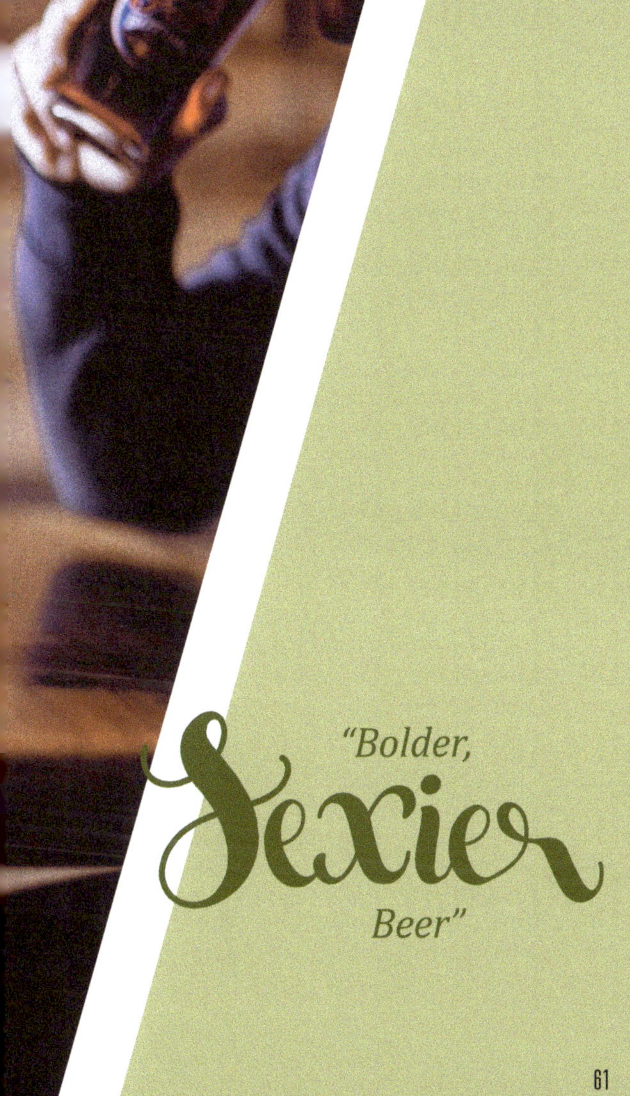

"Bolder,
Sexier
Beer"

Keepin' the Beer Drinkin' Good

An easily recognizable brand, each beer features a pretty woman with an accentuated bottom in a style reminiscent of World War II nose art, as imagery combines with taste to tell a bigger story.

The excellent branding helps sell the beer, but it's their painstakingly perfected styles that sell the brand and keep the drinkin' good. Like their ladies' buttocks, their beer is big, full, and round. Its flavor is fat with personality. And since you can fool people's eyes, but you can't fool their palates, they go to great measures to make sure it is all above par. How do they do it?

Their head brewer cut his teeth at Delaware's Dogfish Head, then took a spin with Foothills Brewing in North Carolina. Talent like that has helped Fat Bottom perfect its catalog of core beers, while delivering creations indicative of Music City's unique flair. Brews run the gamut, like the highly drinkable All-American Ruby Red Ale or the Cinco de Knockout, a surprisingly pleasing, spicy concoction of jalapeños and serrano peppers aged on oak chips. Even Nashville's rich history gets a nod with a special beer brewed using local ingredients from the Hermitage, the home of America's seventh President Andrew Jackson. And every Wednesday on small batch night, who knows, you might be getting a first taste of their next big success.

The laid-back atmosphere and air of camaraderie in the brewpub is quintessential Nashville. But more so, Fat Bottom helps tell the story of keepin' our beer drinkin' good with crafty branding supported by crafty creations. And like us, they hope to share that story with the world.

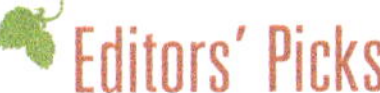

Editors' Picks

Ginger Wheat Ale: (4.6% ABV, 18 IBU)

Ruby Red American Ale: (5.3% ABV, 35 IBU)

Java Jane Coffee Porter: (4.2% ABV, 26 IBU)

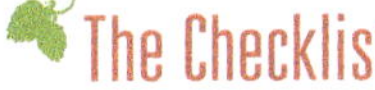

The Checklist

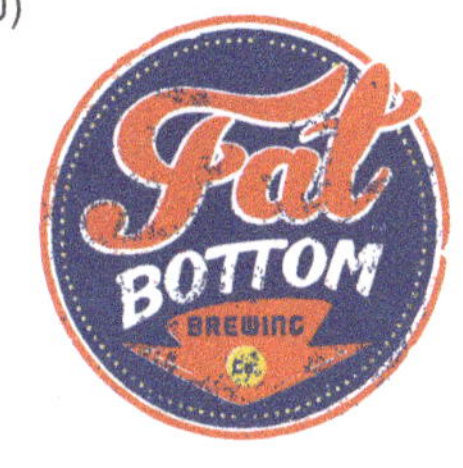

Taproom: Yes

Bottles/Cans: Yes

Availability: All over TN

Website: www.fatbottombrewing.com

What Brew Best Represents You?

Black Betty India Black Ale
(4.4% ABV, 56 IBU) – As mysterious as its muse Betty Paige. If you drink it with your eyes closed, aside from looking like an idiot, you'd be surprised by its color. American hops with German malt give it a full body with smoky flavor.

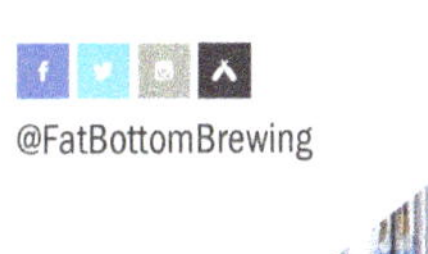

@FatBottomBrewing

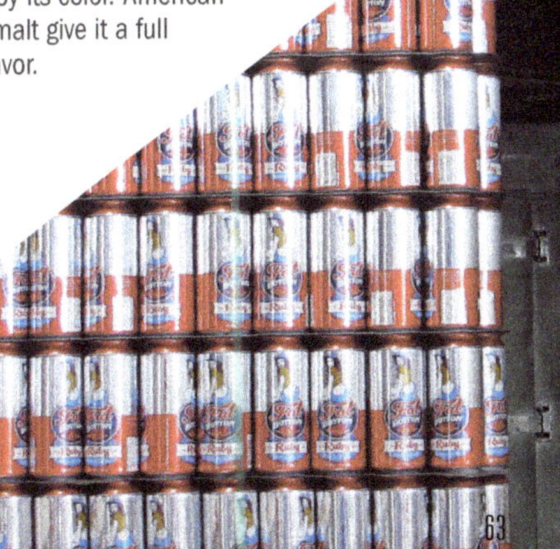

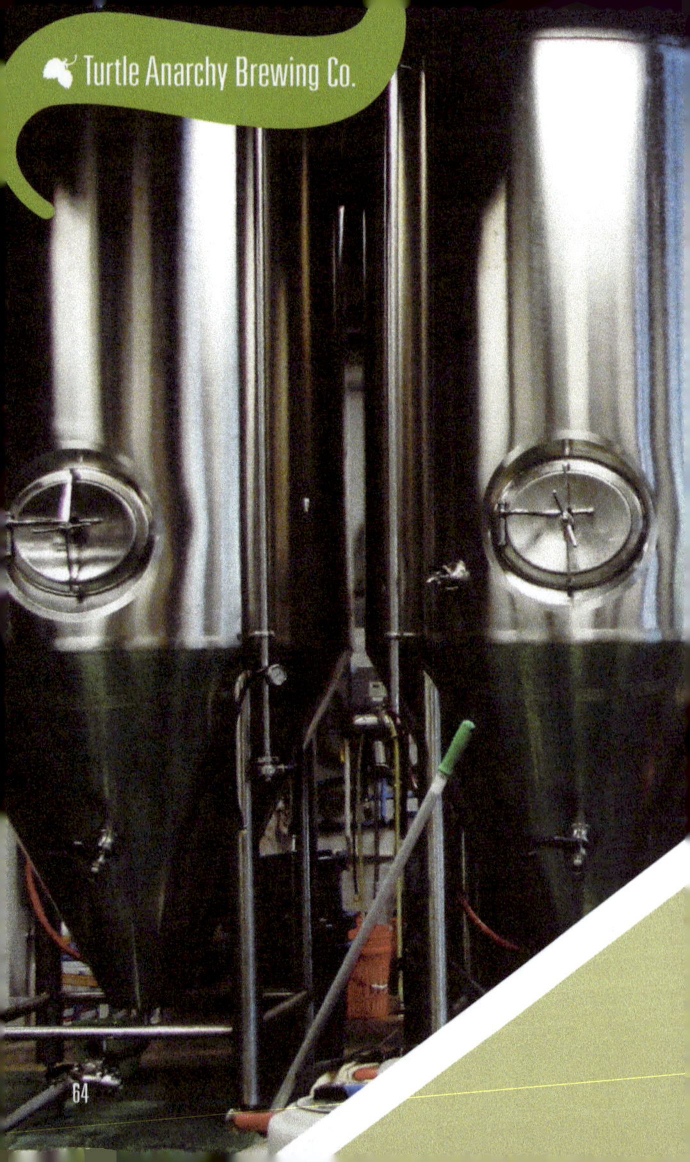
Turtle Anarchy Brewing Co.

"A slow **revolution** *of winning people over to craft beer one pint at a time"*

The Story

As is the case with many who move to Nashville, Turtle Anarchy founder Mark Kamp originally showed up with a plan to enter into the music biz. While studying music publishing at Belmont University, Kamp began brewing his own beer, perfectly timed so it was ready to drink by his twenty-first birthday.

Kamp's plan had always been to open his own business, but upon the arrival of his two younger brothers things started to move in a different direction. Once the Kamp bros began brewing together the floodgates opened up and the beer was flowing free. Before too long they were cranking out five gallons every Saturday (oh, to have friends like that in college). And so it was, the bliss of the homebrew, providing the populace with some good drinkin', won out over a career in publishing easy listenin'.

Upon graduating in 2010 Kamp held an internship at a local craft brewery in town where he learned what it takes to produce beer on a commercial scale. Two years later the entire Kamp family got in on the action and Turtle Anarchy opened up shop in July 2012.

Keepin' the Beer Drinkin' Good

Though the revolution may be slow, the same can't be said about Turtle Anarchy's growth. When first opening, the base of operations was located about twenty miles south of Nashville in historic Franklin, TN. Their three-year plan must have panned out, because in July 2015, exactly three years after rolling out their first keg, the Kamps moved into a new facility, completely tricked out with a canning line, in super-trendy West Nashville.

Another Nashville 100 percent family-owned brewery, Turtle Anarchy is a great example of the young craft beer movement being driven forward by a generation that hasn't really known anything but craft beer. This youthful exuberance is evident in the wide range of styles they take on, pressing the limits without sacrificing who they are. They are winning people over to beer that is drinkin' good by simply brewing the beer they want to brew in a loving way.

It probably helps that they started out sipping on styles that are more comparable to their best-selling Portly Stout, which features three different black malts from the UK for a perfectly blended chocoffee flavor. Not exactly the bright-yellow, watered-down fizzy stuff most of us began with. By stepping out with creative combinations like ginger and juniper or coconut and Thai curry, they give their crafts the slight touches and tweaks that make them unique.

Artfully crafted with love, Turtle Anarchy creates a wide variety of styles with one purpose: to offer Nashville more soldiers that are drinkin' good, so the craft beer revolution can roll on at higher speeds.

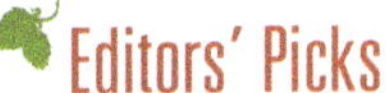

Editors' Picks

Aurumglass: (5.5% ABV, 20 IBU)

Portly Stout: (6.2% ABV, 40 IBU)

Another Way to Rye: (6.2% ABV, 60 IBU)

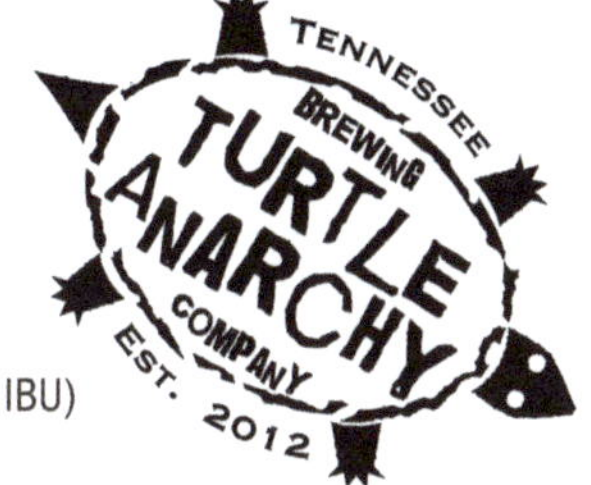

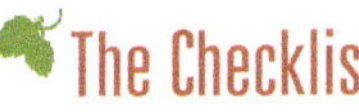

The Checklist

Taproom: No

Bottles/Cans: Yes

Availability: Middle TN and Eastern TN

Website: www.turtleanarchy.com

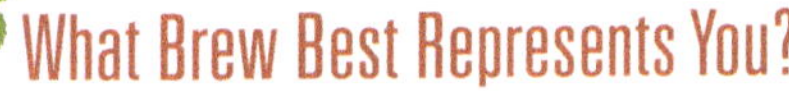

What Brew Best Represents You?

Turtle Anarchy Portly Stout
(6.2% ABV, 40 IBU) – With minimum hops, the roasted malt distinctiveness of this Nashville favorite stands tall and strong along with its perfectly balanced body. Sweet and light, chocolaty with a smidge of ashy flavor.

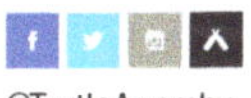

@TurtleAnarchy

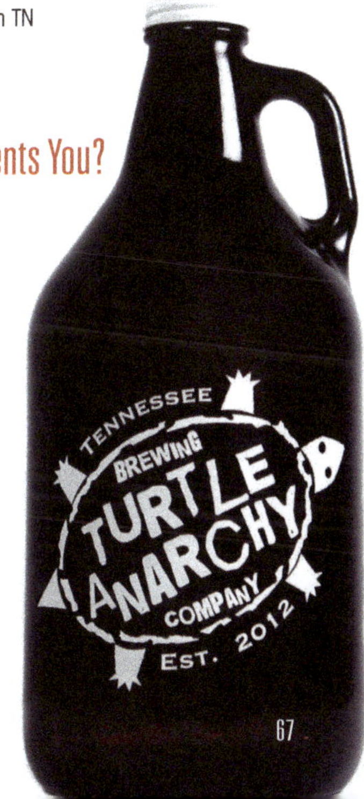

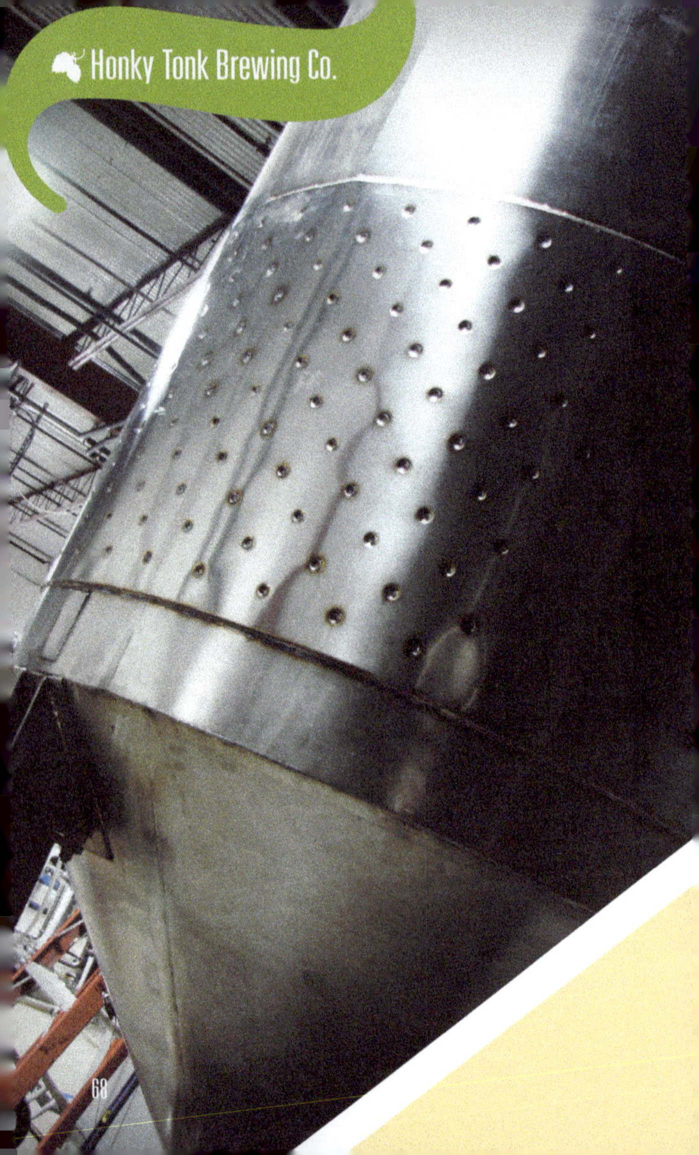

"tuned up lagers and ales"

The Story

Founder, brewer, sales guy, delivery dude Scott Swygert of Honky Tonk Brewing Co. does it all. Before moving to Nashville he resided in Alaska, Oregon, and Colorado, all hotbeds of American craft brewing. So when he decided to begin home brewing he definitely had a nice platform to jump off. Like most of Nashville's pioneering purveyors of craft brews, after a few successful batches he quickly got hooked and decided to turn his love of brewing into a business.

Previous to being the omnipresent face of Honky Tonk, Swygert worked in real estate and also held a license as a contractor. All this came in quite handy when building his new venture, mostly because it was by his own handiwork that Honky Tonk took shape. Swygert, along with a small band of helpers, fabricated every bit of the brewery, from the brewpub to the production facility. It took the better part of two years traveling across the Southeast, scrapping together each bit of Honky Tonk's inner workings, and uncounted hours hammering, cutting, welding, and sweating, until piece-by-piece, the brewery was ready to serve its first beer in October 2014.

Keepin' the Beer Drinkin' Good

The brewery—a medley of Music City's roots and its progressive attitude, in name and practice—is young, but with tons of room to grow. While many brewers may have waited a bit before sharing their wares with the public, Swygert was quick to pull the trigger. The sole owner operates under the guise, if the beer is drinkin' good then what reason is there to wait?

Going at it alone was by no means an easy task. It took Swygert three trips to Alabama just to pick up his massive walk-in cooler. The metal roofing above the bar, taken from an old farm building in Williamson County, took him an entire day to cut, clean, and mount. All of this and more, along with a custom-built stage for live music, deliver a unique blend of rustic character and homey comfort that show why Honky Tonk Brewing Co. is thoroughly handcrafted in every way.

Its location is a bit unconventional, tucked into a business park near Nashville's Metrocenter, but in less than a year the brewery has built a strong following thanks to its simple approach to craft beer. The custom welded fermenting tanks, along with the sudsy goodness contained within, is all courtesy of one guy, who in the end just likes making things. There is no highbrow philosophy here—beer is just fun to make. And if people like it then Swygert will keep making it. Those looking for an indicator of how good the drinkin' is only need note the frequent visitors tally behind the bar. By the looks of it, Honky Tonk will be keeping the beer drinkin' good for a while.

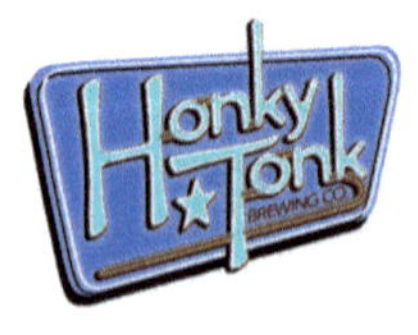

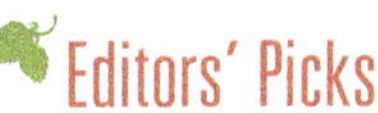

Editors' Picks

Tennessee Jed: (6.2% ABV, 25 IBU)

West Coast IPA: (6.3% ABV, 95 IBU)

Amber Ale: (5.8% ABV, 35 IBU)

The Checklist

Taproom: Yes

Bottles/Cans: Cans coming Fall 2015

Availability: Davidson County

Website: www.facebook.com/HonkyTonkBeer

What Brew Best Represents You?

Hatfield Bold & Smooth Gold Summer Ale
(6.2% ABV, 20 IBU) – A torrential downpour of smooth flavor for your taste buds–named after famous rainmaker Charles Hatfield who, in 1916, was run out of San Diego after supposedly causing a flood that resulted in an estimated $3.5 million in damages.

@HonkyTonkBrewing

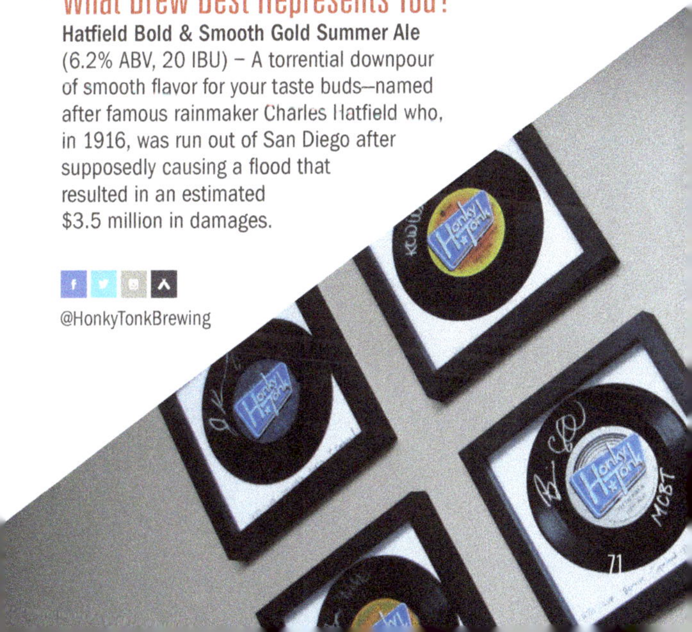

This book is dedicated to the memory of Stephanie Weins, a pillar of the Nashville craft beer community, and all of the creative and crafty, passionate and proud brewers who came before, who have contributed to this fine art in so many different ways. May your intrepid spirits live on forever in glasses full of brews that are drinkin' good. Cheers!

www.ingramcontent.com/pod-product-compliance
Lightning Source LLC
LaVergne TN
LVHW052356100826
845147LV00013B/855

* 9 7 8 1 9 4 3 3 2 8 2 6 0 *